Triumph at Kitty Hawk

Orville and Wilbur Wright, 1910. *Courtesy of the National Air and Space Museum, Washington, D.C.*

THOMAS C. PARRAMORE

Triumph at Kitty Hawk

The Wright Brothers and Powered Flight

OFFICE OF ARCHIVES AND HISTORY
NORTH CAROLINA DEPARTMENT OF CULTURAL RESOURCES
RALEIGH
2003

© 1993 by the North Carolina Division of Archives and History
(3rd printing, 2003)
ISBN 0-86526-259-4

Cover: The Wright brothers visited the North Carolina Outer Banks three times to experiment with glider flying before they made the first powered flight in 1903. The cover shows Wilbur making a right turn in their glider at Kill Devil Hills in October 1902. *Courtesy of the Library of Congress, Washington, D.C.*

Contents

Foreword

For more than thirty years the Historical Publications Section kept in print a brief pamphlet titled *The Wright Brothers and Their Development of the Airplane* by Barbara Craig. Through eight printings it sold more than thirty thousand copies. Its popularity demonstrated the fascination with which the public continues to view the accomplishments of Wilbur and Orville Wright at Kitty Hawk. In the past four decades several important new studies about the history of powered flight have appeared that have deepened appreciation for the Wright brothers' technological innovation and ingenuity. Unlike many inventors, the Dayton bicycle makers kept detailed records of their trials, errors, and experiments, and historians have analyzed those records extensively. But a part of the story was still missing.

Drawing on the most recent scholarship and his own thorough knowledge of Tar Heel sources, Thomas C. Parramore, professor emeritus at Meredith College, has written an account of the Wright brothers' exploits at Kitty Hawk from a North Carolina perspective. Through an examination of local sources (many scattered and obscure), research in the Wrights' papers (both published and unpublished) as well as other manuscript sources, and interviews with descendants of the families on the Outer Banks who assisted the Wrights, Dr. Parramore has told for the first time how North Carolinians perceived the odd Ohioans. The Wrights also left amusing accounts of the provincialism and isolation of the Outer Banks at the turn of the twentieth century. But overall deep friendship and mutual respect between the dogged inventors and hardy Bankers were forged on the windblown slopes of Kill Devil Hills.

Tom Parramore needs no introduction to devotees of North Carolina history. For more than four decades he has been one of the state's most versatile historians, publishing textbooks, monographs, and articles on a wide range of subjects. His article "The Tuscarora Ascendancy" won the 1983 R. D. W. Connor Award as the best article to appear in the *North Carolina Historical Review* that year. In addition to serving a five-year term on the *Review*'s Advisory Editorial Committee, Dr. Parramore has been elected president of both the Historical Society of North Carolina and the North Carolina Literary and Historical Association. Dr. Parramore

received his undergraduate and graduate education at the University of
North Carolina at Chapel Hill.

Ann W. Little did the preliminary editing on the manuscript for this
book, and Sandra T. Hall entered the material on a computer for production on a desktop publishing system. Kathleen B. Wyche took time from
her busy schedule as editor of the *North Carolina Historical Review* to
design, lay out, and typeset the book electronically. Lisa D. Bailey assisted
with the proofreading. To all who contributed to the timely publication
of this book, sincere gratitude is extended.

Donna E. Kelly
Historical Publications Administrator

September 2003

Acknowledgments

The preparation of this book provided the author with opportunities to become acquainted with numerous descendants of those Outer Bankers who, in so many ways, assisted the Wright brothers. He has found them to be as gracious, hospitable, and helpful as did the Dayton bicycle mechanics of the first years of the twentieth century. Many were not only willing but eager to share family reminiscences, clippings, photographs, letters, albums, and other memorabilia, to permit inspection of precious relics of Wright gliders and airplanes, and to help the work along in other ways.

The author is especially indebted to Daniel Grady Tate, grandson of Dan Tate and son of Tom Tate, for sharing useful family data and stories, reviewing the manuscript, and encouragement in the project. In addition, much valuable information was passed along by Iva Tate Jordan, Ruth Tate, Madge Daniels Barbour, Lois Daniels Smith, Mellie Daniels Pearce, Adam Dough Etheridge IV, Willie Joliffe, Alma Etheridge Wilson, and Willa Severn Raye, among others.

Also, the services and assistance of Dawne Dewey of the Wright State University Archives; Wynne Dough, former curator of the Outer Banks History Center; Robert Mason, formerly of the Norfolk *Virginian-Pilot*, and the competent and conscientious staff of the Historical Publications Section and its former head, Jeffrey J. Crow, are gratefully acknowledged.

Finally, the author owes a particular debt to Bill Harris of the National Park Service for pointing out a number of errors in the 1993 printing of this volume. Mr. Harris, a grandson of Elijah W. Baum, interviewed a number of Outer Banks residents who, like his grandfather, had known the Wright brothers. Tapes of his interviews are available at the Outer Banks History Center, Manteo, North Carolina.

CHAPTER ONE

Aviation in North Carolina before 1903

The Kitty Hawkers

When Orville Wright first swooped skyward from a North Carolina sand dune in late 1903, he was not introducing the concept of human flight to incredulous Tar Heel bystanders. The traditional version of the Wright brothers' first flight ignores the fact that Outer Banks residents and North Carolinians in general had become accustomed to the idea that human flight was in the offing. Many had watched the Wrights' gliders in action for over three years. Opinions did vary, however, on the Wright brothers' role in the quickly evolving technology of aviation.

Even Kitty Hawk's Bill Tate—one of numerous North Carolina associates of the Wrights—in retrospect downplayed local support for the Wrights' venture. Late in his life, he wrote a magazine piece in which he declared that "99 per cent. and .99 of the other per cent. of the world back in 1900 to 1903 simply believed [the Wrights] to be a pair of harmless nuts." Kitty Hawkers, he wrote, believed "that if it had been intended that man should fly, he would already be flying, or at least wing feathers would have been growing on his shoulders."[1]

But perhaps Tate only meant to congratulate himself in a subtle way for his own unshakable faith in the Wright brothers. In October 1900 Orville Wright had written that this same Kitty Hawker was so enthusiastic about flying that he "would like to spend his remaining days . . . in experimenting with flying machines."[2] Bill Tate, in fact, was won over to airplanes more than three years before one actually flew. A closer look at his turn-of-the-century world, moreover, reveals a situation quite otherwise than Bill remembered it. North Carolina provides a prime illustration.

At the opening of the twentieth century, folks living along the state's rugged Atlantic fringe were well aware that balloonists often made manned (and "womaned") flights at Norfolk, Virginia, about fifty miles north of Kitty Hawk. Such exhibitions, usually well publicized, had been performed there for well over a century. Older residents could recall that balloons were also used at Hampton Roads by Union army spotters during the Civil War to observe Confederate camps and troop movements around Norfolk.[3]

In addition, Currituck and Dare County residents who attended the annual state fairs at Raleigh had seen such flights. They had even watched balloonists parachute safely from hundreds of feet in the sky. For enraptured throngs, balloons soaring majestically out of sight among the clouds offered a spectacle that no sand-skimming contraption of wood and muslin was likely to match. Ballooning, whether by gas or hot air, was well known to virtually all Carolinians by 1903. Kitty Hawk residents wishing to see men fly in the fall of 1903 needed only to take a two-dollar boat ride to Elizabeth City to watch parachuting balloonists at the Albemarle Fair.[4]

Maneuvers performed by balloons could very likely be imitated with the queer sort of kite that the Wrights began experimenting with on the Outer Banks in the fall of 1900. Kitty Hawkers followed the Wright experiments with interest and a growing sense of anticipation. It would be exciting if the brothers succeeded in flying their machine, but the accomplishment would not be totally unexpected. Orville should not have been too disappointed if the locals, on the whole, took his first flight in stride. He would have to accept the fact that housewives peering through their windows were chiefly interested in the effect the noisy machine had on their chickens and livestock. After all, residents of the Outer Banks had watched the Wrights fly gliders for over three years. Some observers preferred the first machines—the quiet ones, without the obnoxious motors.

Some Tar Heel Aeronauts

By 1903 at least half a dozen Tar Heels—and probably somewhat more than that—had tried to build airships of their own. Several of them were still at it when the Wrights were experimenting at Kitty Hawk. One of these, young John M. Smith from the Beaufort County hamlet of Pantego, lived just seventy miles southwest of Kitty Hawk. (Even today, Smith's descendants speak darkly of "two well-dressed travelling men" who stole his clockwork model and blueprints out of his barn one night in 1897. According to them, the clandestine operation led directly to the successful 1903 flights at Kill Devil Hill!)[5]

As the insinuations indicate, the Wrights were not the only owners of airships in North Carolina. In a Hertford County ginhouse (about a hundred miles west of Kitty Hawk) in the summer of 1900—perhaps by then enveloped in rust and spider webs—sat James Henry Gatling's twin-propellered monoplane. It had wings, a tail, and an "elevator" not altogether unlike the Wright Flyer. Norfolk and Raleigh newspapers called attention to this machine in the early 1870s, while it was still under construction. Henry Gatling, a patenting inventor, began to experiment with flying after designing practical equipment and new techniques to make farming more productive.[6]

Henry, the older brother of Gatling gun inventor Richard J. Gatling, actually hand cranked his airplane off the ginhouse roof one Sunday afternoon in 1873 and flew a hundred feet before crashing. He was said to have considered installing an electric motor after that, but his experiments ended when he was murdered in 1879. The plane had not flown again since 1873. In the thirty years between then and 1903, however, it was available—if some gifted mechanic had decided to pursue Gatling's dream.[7]

James Henry Gatling (1816-1879), older brother of Gatling gun inventor Richard J. Gatling and a farmer of the Maney's Neck section of Hertford County, N.C., in 1872 built a hand-powered flying machine and flew it for about one hundred feet off his gin-mill roof. A wing struck a tree and the machine crashed, with only minor injury to the builder. Artist Bill Ballard depicted Gatling and his machine at the Gatling farm. *Courtesy of the late F. Roy Johnson.*

Then there was Dr. Daniel Asbury, a kinsman of the celebrated Methodist bishop Francis Asbury. In 1881, he tried—and failed—to fly his Bird-Machine from his Mecklenburg County farm (at what is now Douglas International Airport) to Independence Square in Charlotte, a distance of seven miles. Asbury, a prolific inventor whose method of flue-curing tobacco was still in use in 1903 in much of Virginia and North Carolina, had built a cylindrical hot-air balloon with canvas wings.[8]

Dr. Asbury's idea was to sit in a basket carried under the balloon and use pedals to make the wings flap him off the ground. Once airborne, he would achieve forward motion by pedaling a shaft driving twin propellers attached to the basket. He died in 1882, while putting final touches on his invention. Although it is unlikely that this pedal balloon ever received a trial of its aerodynamic capabilities, rumors that it had flown were still circulating in the Charlotte area as late as 1903.[9]

Henry Gatling and Daniel Asbury represented a preindustrial age in North Carolina when no form of reliable artificial power existed for moving a machine along the roads, let alone through the skies. But such forms were soon to appear and, when they did, they energized Tar Heel inventors for a new assault on the dream of heavier-than-air flight. Elizabeth City resident Fred Proctor was one of those who, before the end of the nineteenth century, was predicting that "ships would be built to sail in the air."[10]

Horseless Carriages in the Air

In the 1880s the aeronautical world accepted Frenchman Clement Ader's conclusion that unaided human muscles could not furnish enough power to sustain an airplane in flight. Short hops of this kind were finally achieved by 1921; the pedal-powered *Gossamer Albatross* flew the English Channel in 1979.[11] Some would-be aeronauts, North Carolinians included, supposed that flight was impossible without a balloon filled with hot air or gas, though a motor would be necessary to make an airship go in the direction one wished. Others continued to nourish Henry Gatling's notion that flight might be possible even without a balloon, provided that the right kind of motor could be found to furnish the power.

At the turn of the twentieth century, there were at least four Tar Heel contemporaries of the Wrights who were pursuing one or the other of those two lines of investigation. Pantego's John M. Smith had plenty of competition.

A main issue with aeronauts of the time was what kind of artificial power could best serve the purpose of driving an aircraft. By 1901 there were a few horseless carriages on the streets of North Carolina towns, including several built by native craftsmen. Some ran on gasoline, others by steam or electricity.[12] Any of these kinds of motors, if sufficiently light and powerful, might also plausibly drive an airplane or a dirigible (steerable) balloon. In France, Brazilian aeronaut Alberto Santos-Dumont struggled heroically to make his gasoline-powered air bag move in the direction that he—not the wind—chose. But his efforts had not been successful by 1901.

Jacob Aaron Hill (1862-1927). "Jake" Hill, formerly a Stokes County tenant farmer, built a gasoline-powered dirigible airship in 1902. It apparently never flew but spent years in a shed behind the Winston home to which he moved in that year. Hill is shown here, presumably during the 1890s, in his early thirties. *Courtesy of his grandson, Rev. W. Stephen King.*

In 1903 in a woodshop in Winston stood Jake and William Hill's sleek new dirigible, to all appearances ready to cast off for a flight among the stars. The machine had an air bag about thirty feet long, with a light gasoline motor attached to its undercarriage. It also had a set of four parasols extending from the undercarriage to catch the wind and guide it once aloft.[13]

Jake Hill, lately a Stokes County tenant farmer and principal builder of the airship, sold stock in his machine to raise money for his experiments. He expected eventually to raise more money by selling tickets to those who came to watch him fly. He planned to take his machine to the Louisiana Purchase Centennial at St. Louis in 1904 and compete for a one-hundred-thousand-dollar grand prize for the best airship there. The *Charlotte Observer* in May 1903 judged him about ready to launch his first flight and predicted success for him. For unknown reasons, however, Jake apparently never got airborne—despite the report in a 1903 Norfolk *Virginian-Pilot* indicating that he did.[14]

At Reidsville, a short distance northeast of Winston, Louis Kromm by early 1902 was inviting fellow citizens to drop by to see the model of the three-engined airship in which he proposed to deliver the government mails. Scoffers had to contend with the spectacle of Fletcher Waynick's new homemade horseless carriage (Reidsville's first) roaring up and down the streets and clattering off on trips to Burlington and Greensboro. A decade earlier, few of them would have thought that possible either.[15]

Kromm was a native of Baltimore who worked for a Reidsville manufacturer of horse-collar pads. His invention was truly a heavier-than-air machine—with three decks (for passengers, machinery, and cargo), "lighted throughout" by electricity, and all driven by what he described as a perpetual-motion engine. The full-sized plane was to be built on Reidsville's athletic field. Like Jake Hill, Kromm announced that he intended to enter his craft in the St. Louis Exposition. But nothing came of his plans; Kromm soon gave up his project and returned to his native Baltimore.[16]

The Case of Dr. Christmas

By late 1903, none of the aspiring Tar Heel aeronauts had succeeded in flying either a dirigible or an airplane. But one of them, William Wallace Whitney Christmas, was nearing success and was to become reportedly the first American after the Wright brothers to build and fly a plane. Christmas came from a well-known family in North Carolina. His great-uncle, William Christmas, had surveyed and laid off the city of Raleigh.[17]

William W. W. Christmas was born at Warrenton in 1865 and moved with his father, sister, and two brothers to Washington, D.C., soon after his mother's death in 1879. He was educated first at the University of Virginia and later at George Washington University, where he obtained a medical degree. He got into aeronautics while practicing medicine in Washington in 1898. Apparently, he became associated with Professor Samuel P. Langley—then America's leading aeronautics expert—and he began building and flying gliders in 1905.[18]

Early in 1908 Dr. Christmas constructed and tested a gasoline-driven biplane, the *Red Bird*. On March 8, 1908, he is said to have flown his machine for about a hundred feet across a field near Fairfax Station, Virginia, making a successful forty-five-degree turn. He made several other flights in the following week, one for about half a mile. An invention Christmas patented in 1914, the inset aileron, is still considered to be fundamental for the control of airplanes in flight.[19]

Dr. Christmas built a number of planes in later years and was to remain closely associated with the development of aviation for the next half century. In 1960, after his death in Manhattan at age ninety-four, the *New York Times* credited him with over three hundred inventions, more than one hundred of them in the field of aeronautics. There were those who thought his work in aviation second only to the Wrights' in importance.[20]

The Wright brothers, therefore, did not attempt anything on North Carolina soil that had not been tried before. What they and Dr. Christmas understood by 1903 was that power was not the main problem holding back success for airplanes. The real obstacle was control of a plane once it was in the air. Several kinds of powerful motors were available for the purpose of flying once the problem of control was mastered.

A few European and American experimenters had already felt the momentary thrill of being lifted a few feet or inches off the ground in their airplanes, but none had figured out how to steer or balance them after that. If the pilots could not balance and guide their machines, they would quickly tilt or wobble themselves into the dirt. As the new century began, this was the problem that Dr. Christmas and the Wrights were studying. Soon all three would solve it.

Aeronautical Poets and Journalists

Other Tar Heels demonstrated their faith that man would fly someday. Although probably unknown to the Wrights, William Henry Rhodes had rhapsodized on the glories of powered flight shortly before Wilbur was born. Rhodes was well known in North Carolina as the author of a popular book of verse entitled *The Indian Gallows and Other Poems.* His father had served as American consul in the Republic of Texas.[21]

In the early stages of the Gold Rush, William Henry Rhodes had traveled to California. In the 1860s Rhodes wrote two poems in celebration of dirigible experiments then being conducted in that state. A native of Windsor, within a day's boat ride of Kitty Hawk, Rhodes boasted in early 1867 that

> Today man masters earth, and sea, and air,
> Subdues all nature to his ruling care,
> Flies back to EDEN, where his fathers trod,
> Spurns neath his feet the globe—and faces God![22]

If the Wrights had subscribed to the *Charlotte Observer*, they would have seen frequent editorials predicting that humans would soon fly. One of the strongest proponents of powered flight in all of newspaper journalism, the *Charlotte Observer* kept close track of aeronautical experimenters in Europe and America. The paper applauded Samuel P. Langley's accomplishment in 1896, when his large steam-driven model plane flew briefly over the Potomac River. Mankind appeared to be on the verge of realizing a primal dream.[23]

By late 1903, however, Langley's machine experienced a succession of humiliating crashes. It seemed clear that Langley was not, after all, destined to be the first human to fly. But the *Charlotte Observer* still held out high hopes for others, including Stokes County's Jake Hill and his dirigible. Editor Daniel Tompkins predicted boldly in May 1903 that Hill—or someone else—would soon "cleave the air" in a flying machine.[24]

Mystery Airships

Many eastern North Carolinians were convinced that they had already seen powered aircraft sailing across their horizons. In April 1897 much of the Coastal Plain was aflutter over the appearance of what seemed to be a cigar-shaped airship, often moving at very high speeds. Residents of Wilmington, Williamston, Kenly, Fayetteville, Lumberton, Chadbourn, and other towns reported having seen an airborne vehicle with ropes and rigging dangling from it, brilliant lights, the tinkling of bells coming from inside—even men clinging to the rigging.[25]

Some Tar Heel newspapers speculated that the mysterious vehicle might be a visitor from Mars. Others, like the *Wilmington Messenger*, suggested it was more likely "an aerial ship sent up as an experiment by some ingenious inventor." There were reports of such airships from coast to coast in 1896 and 1897, probably the first mass sightings of UFOs.[26] In the late nineteenth century—amid demonstrations of boxes that sang and talked, pictures that moved, carriages that ran without horses, lights that required no flame, and conversations between people hundreds of miles apart—airplanes had ceased to be unthinkable.

And what of premonitions? In 1874 Bald Mountain, near the Rutherford-McDowell County line, began emitting eerie roars that its neighbors feared might signal a volcanic eruption. (The mountain is still called Rumbling Bald.) French novelist Jules Verne a decade later used these rumblings in a tale of mad scientist Robur's North Carolina terror machine—able to travel on land, sea, and in the air—built deep inside the mountain.[27] (The spelling *Orbur*, conflating *Orville* and *Wilbur*, would have given Verne's novel a quality of startling prophesy!)

What follows is the story of the first two human beings to build and fly a successful airplane, thus inaugurating a great new age in human travel and communication—and, sorrowfully, death and destruction. But it is also the story of the major role played in that success by North Carolinians, scores of whom made important contributions to the efforts of the Wrights. An examination of that role makes it uncertain whether the

Wrights would have succeeded in some other place, without the hospitable and accommodating people of the Outer Banks. From 1900 through 1903, the genius of the Wrights was—necessarily—complemented by the labors, services, and interest of many people, the majority of whom were Tar Heels.

CHAPTER TWO

Appointment at Kitty Hawk

Genius in Their Genes?

Biographers have been hard pressed to explain the success of the Wright brothers in solving one of the greatest puzzles of human thought. That puzzle had stumped all the great minds of the past who studied it, Leonardo da Vinci among them. It had also baffled such contemporaries of the Wrights as Alexander Graham Bell, Thomas A. Edison, and Hiram Maxim—all geniuses of the industrial age. The closer one looks at the Wrights, the more intriguing the mystery of their achievement becomes.

It would be satisfying if certain life circumstances of the pioneers of aviation could be offered by way of explanation. Wilbur and Orville were sons of the Reverend Milton Wright, a minister (and later bishop) of the United Brethren church, and his wife, Susan Koerner Wright. Wilbur was born on April 16, 1867, while his father was stationed in Millville, Indiana; Orville was born on August 19, 1871, in Dayton, Ohio. They also had older brothers, Reuchlin and Lorin, and a younger sister, Katharine (Kate).[1]

The younger brothers were to grow to manhood in a cozy household where they were loved and respected, although they had achieved nothing particularly noteworthy as they entered the fourth decade of their lives. Although Reuchlin and Lorin married and left home at appropriate ages to start their own households, Wilbur and Orville stayed behind, catering to the needs of their parents and sister and, in turn, being nurtured by them. Neither ended his formal education with so much as a high school diploma, though the other siblings attended college. They showed no interest in young women or in starting their own families—and never would. As late as the year 1900, when Wilbur had little more than a decade to live, neither had ventured far from the restricted region of their upbringing or had done anything worth citing in a county or municipal history.[2]

This limited experience of the outside world suggests the possibility that genetic inheritance may better explain the mechanical talent of the

Wrights. The surname itself, of course, signifies that some paternal forebear—possibly a maker of carts or wheels or boats—had also been mechanically gifted. But it was more obviously from their maternal side that they inherited mechanical aptitude. Susan K. Wright is said to have been very resourceful in converting common household utensils into tools and in designing, making, and mending clothes. She once even built a sled for her children. Her father, German immigrant John G. Koerner, had been a manufacturer of carriages and farm wagons. So it may have come naturally to the Wright boys to interest themselves in mechanical things.[3]

A Taste of Ink

Although Wilbur and Orville were good students at the grammar and high schools in the various towns where their father held pulpits, neither stayed in school long enough to graduate. Higher education was deemed necessary only for those entering a learned profession such as law, medicine, or the ministry. Wilbur sometimes had notions of pursuing a college degree to become a teacher or preacher, but he never followed up on it. Both boys read widely, however, from their family's extensive collection of periodicals and books and at local libraries. Wilbur, especially, was an avid reader, leaning toward the novels of Sir Walter Scott, history, theology, literature, the sciences, and encyclopedia articles.[4]

Nevertheless, the brothers clearly found more satisfaction in working with their hands. Their mechanical interests were shown early in building a wooden lathe, their first serious project together. Enlisted to fold copies of a weekly church newspaper published by his father, Wilbur invented a gadget that helped him do so more rapidly. Later, the boys became skillful enough as carpenters to put a front porch on the family home and do extensive remodeling of the interior.[5] There was a certain precocious cleverness in this sort of thing, but nothing suggesting any particular direction their lives might take or any small contribution they might make to the human condition.

At age twelve, in 1883, Orville became interested in wood engraving and fashioned from the spring of a pocketknife a tool to help him make woodcuts. He ran the prints off on his father's press until the next Christmas, when Wilbur presented him with a set of engraving tools. For a while the brothers appeared to have stumbled onto something productive to do with their lives.[6]

From engraving, it was a short step to printing. When Orville found that a friend, Ed Sines, owned a small printing press, he joined with him to form a mock company, Sines and Wright. The partners rigged a telegraph line between their homes—though it does not seem to have worked very reliably. Orville would later build for himself a new kind of calculating machine that multiplied as well as added and subtracted. Also, he tried to build a simplified kind of typewriter.[7]

Before long, Orville's father gave him a larger press. The partners then printed a single issue of a newspaper called the *Midget*, intended for fellow eighth graders. They soon found, however, that some local merchants would pay to have placards, brochures, and other kinds of advertising printed for their customers. Sines and Wright set up business in the Wrights' barn, but Orville quickly bought out his partner and ran the press himself. After building a larger press, he worked for two summers with local professional printers to learn more about the business.[8]

Wilbur likewise showed some interest in printing, but at age eighteen he suffered a disabling accident. He had always been a fine athlete—perhaps the best gymnast in the community—and an enthusiastic participant in baseball, hockey, and the local version of football. In March 1885 he was struck in the face with a hockey stick, knocking out most of his front teeth and confining him at home for a long period. He also had chronic stomach trouble and a worrisome heart condition.[9]

With Mrs. Wright having grown ill before the accident and bedridden by 1887, Wilbur now spent much of his time attending to her needs. He was dealt another blow in July 1889, when she died of tuberculosis. Wilbur, who had always been very close to his mother, seemed briefly to slip further into his shell of isolation. But, as his own health improved, he began showing once more a zest for living.[10]

There was talk in the family of sending Wilbur to Yale Divinity School to prepare him for the ministry. In the spring of 1888 he appeared to take a step in that direction by composing and publishing a controversial pamphlet taking Bishop Wright's side in a dispute within the United Brethren church. His first serious published work (followed by other related pieces in the church paper) argued that the Brethren should bar from membership persons belonging to the Freemasons or other secret societies. His intellectual bent was undeniable, but Wilbur always found some excuse for not cultivating it by attending college. He was obviously having a difficult time focusing on any particular work or profession, and it bothered him a great deal.[11]

By early 1889 Orville, aided now by Wilbur, had built a still larger printing press. Renting a small shop, they began publishing a weekly newspaper called the *West-Side News* on March 1. Wilbur, soon distinguished as "editor" (Orville was "publisher"), wrote editorials calling for better streets and sidewalks in the Dayton west side. Among his causes were the defense of woman's suffrage and opposition to American expansion overseas (Hawaii and Cuba were much in the news). A black friend, Paul Laurence Dunbar, later a celebrated poet, contributed some verses to the paper. The press also gained some business in printing religious tracts, annual church reports, club directories, handbills, business cards, and such.[12]

Over the next five years the firm of Wright and Wright also turned out two short-lived newspapers (the *Evening Item* and *Snapshots*) and at least three issues of the *Tattler*, a paper Dunbar started for Dayton's black community. One *Tattler* article dealt with Chicagoan E. J. Pennington's construction of a dirigible airship. But the Wrights found that a small journal dependent on neighborhood trade was no match for Dayton's twelve established papers. Subscriptions and job-printing, in fact, barely met the expenses of the operation. The Wrights were left with scarcely any profit.[13] A national depression that began in 1893 made the outlook for the future bleak.

Bicycles Built by Two

In the early 1890s Wilbur and Orville, growing bored with printing, turned to a new business, bicycles. By then the country was in the throes of a craze for the new European-type "safety" bicycle—with both wheels the same size and chain driven. The first American model had gone on the market in 1887; by 1895 production would reach well over a million a year. Orville bought his first safety bike in 1892, and Wilbur got one soon afterward. The younger brother began competing in track racing, winning several local events. Requests by friends to repair their machines soon led the Wrights into the business of bicycle repairs and sales. Meanwhile, Orville continued to conduct his lethargic job-printing business until he sold it in 1898.[14]

The Wrights' involvement with bicycles soon became more intense. Business improved enough to require the Wright Cycle Company to move three times into larger quarters. At one point in 1893, Wilbur and Orville tried out a set of balloon tires on one of their bikes—perhaps the first time this kind of tire had been used on a vehicle. Their repair work provided them with the know-how to begin in 1896 building their own line of bicycles, the Van Cleve. Later they produced the less expensive St. Clair and Wright Special models. Several hundred of these were built and sold over a period of about five years. In 1895 the brothers converted two old high-wheeler, or "ordinary," bikes they received in trades into a unique and odd-looking two-seater. It required considerable skill to ride—and created a stir wherever they rode it.[15]

Repairing and building bicycles provided the Wrights with opportunities to design and construct power machinery for their shop. They built their own internal-combustion engine for powering their equipment, an

electrical welding device for making frames, and a new type of wheel hub and coaster brake for their cycles. (This kind of technical experience would be important to them later in building gliders and helping to design their first airplane's gasoline engine, when they were unable to buy a suitable one.) In mid-1896 a friend of Orville's, Cordy Ruse, built Dayton's first horseless carriage. Orville spent hours riding in the machine, examining its workings, and discussing with its builder the intricacies of carburetors, gears, and the like.[16]

The bicycle business was a seasonal one, active in spring and summer but dropping off after that. On the lookout for something to occupy his time more fully, Orville approached Wilbur with the idea of manufacturing automobiles. Wilbur's discouraging response killed the notion: "Why it would be easier," he is supposed to have said, "to build a flying machine."[17]

Orville (*opposite*) and Wilbur Wright, Dayton bicycle makers, first became intrigued with the possibility of powered flight in 1899. By 1900 they were searching for an appropriate place to conduct tests of "scientific kite flying." The Outer Banks of North Carolina proved to be a hospitable site. *Courtesy of the National Air and Space Museum, Washington, D.C.*

Birds of a Feather

Was it, perhaps, some psychological predisposition that set the Wright brothers' minds to thoughts of flying? Although Wilbur and Orville had been no closer to one another in childhood than most siblings generally are, strong bonds of mutual trust and affection were forged between them as they approached manhood. They enjoyed one another's company, shared a great many common interests, and found that they could try out their ideas on one another, often with productive results. In a sense, it was a strange partnership, since their personalities strongly contrasted with one another.

Orville, a natty dresser, was friendly, impulsive, ever the optimist, a charming conversationalist. He was liked by nearly all who met him despite a conspicuous and lifelong shyness among strangers. In adulthood, his timidity made him a poor public speaker. His older brother was quiet, cool, a somewhat withdrawn and reserved person, a brooding intellectual. Given to depression as a boy, he managed to overcome it and, in the process, become a notably outgoing and self-possessed man. He had no patience with small talk and, in company, could become totally absorbed with thoughts that cut him off from all that went on around him. Strangers not infrequently interpreted his reserve as arrogance or coldness, but he had an engaging dry wit that softened his somber demeanor.[18]

Some biographers hint that the Wrights were like sparrows, born for flight. After Wilbur became a famous inventor, one writer who met him commented that his long and bony head, prematurely bald, had the look of a bird with a long nose. Another spoke of his "keen, observant, hawklike eyes." Such appraisals implied that the very soul of Wilbur, at least, was at one with the feathered denizens of the sky. They also call to mind John T. Daniels, a Tar Heel who observed both Wrights at close range during parts of 1902 and 1903. He came to "admire the way they could move their arms this way and that and bend their elbows and wrist bones up and down and every which a way, just like the gannets [large seabirds] moved their wings."[19] As an explanation for the Wrights' aerial success, however, these analogies seem less than persuasive.

In light of later events, certain small incidents in the boys' background gained perhaps undue attention from their biographers. Wilbur, for example, was fascinated as a five-year-old with a gyroscopic top he received as a birthday gift. It could be balanced, spinning, on a knife blade. The problem of balance, it has been said, was precisely the one the Wrights were called upon to solve before powered flight was possible; it is also an ingredient in the operation of bicycles. More obviously pertinent is the fact that Orville for a while built his own kites, several of which he sold to neighborhood children.[20]

What might seem in retrospect a turning point in the boys' lives was a gift from their father of a toy helicopter sometime in the late 1870s. An ingenious little machine made of cork, bamboo, and paper, it could be propelled to the ceiling of the Wright home by a twisted rubber band. Wilbur was prompted to make larger models, only to find that each enlargement worked less satisfactorily than the one before. The problem, unrecognizable by him at the time, was that each doubling of size required a geometrical increase (by eight times) of its power. In later life the brothers alternately affirmed and denied that the toy had anything to do with their interest in aviation, although Wilbur did concede a "passive interest" in the subject from childhood.[21] The influence of the toy helicopter is debatable at best.

Otto's Flights

In the early autumn of 1894, the Wrights read an article in a popular magazine, *McClure's*, about German glider expert Otto Lilienthal. Not only was Lilienthal, a trained engineer, the first person to achieve sustained flight in a glider; but he had done so some two thousand times, reaching altitudes of sixty-five feet and distances of over three hundred yards. To the enthusiastic Dayton cycle builders, it was obvious that Lilienthal had invented a sport that surpassed all others for thrills and challenges. They agreed almost at once that they must try to build a glider like Lilienthal's and share his exhilaration.[22]

It was apparent from the *McClure's* article that Lilienthal's success with his gliders must be credited to the shape of the wings. His twenty-foot wings were described as light, ribbed frames of split willow, muslin covered, with a gentle concave curve, or camber, front edge to back, much like those of birds. (If one were to cup an outstretched hand slightly, palm down, the fingertips would be the wing's front edge.) This curving somehow gave his wings a remarkable lifting power, though even Lilienthal was unsure why. The builder had also learned to coat the wings with a gluelike liquid to make them impervious to air. Another key feature of his glider was a rear rudder consisting of horizontal and vertical blades designed to help compensate for sudden imbalances caused by wind gusts.[23]

Lilienthal's flights were always in a straight line; he could change direction only slightly without suffering a fall. Balance, the pilot's main concern once airborne, was maintained by the dangling aeronaut's shifting his body from one side to the other as needed. To begin a flight, Lilienthal carried his glider to the top of an appropriate hill. Climbing under his machine, he took hold of a bar at the leading edge of its wings, stood awaiting a freshening of the breeze, ran a few steps downhill when it came, and launched himself with a final leap. The process was almost identical to hang-gliding techniques of later generations, though so novel at the time that it seemed extraordinary to those who watched him.[24]

Wilbur, the more technically insightful of the brothers, quickly recognized a shortcoming of the Lilienthal machine: that the shifting of the pilot's body for balance would work only with small wings. Larger ones, for greater height and distance, were likely to be uncontrollable in sudden gusts or changing air pressure that the shifting of the pilot's body could not counteract. Yet gliding could not advance beyond Lilienthal's limited success unless the wings could be made larger. The defect seemed to be confirmed during an August 1896 flight when Lilienthal's machine abruptly stalled and nosed over, killing the valiant aeronaut. Since Orville had recently become dangerously ill with typhoid fever, Wilbur waited for his recovery before informing him of Lilienthal's death.[25]

The Powernauts

By the early spring of 1899, when Orville was fully recovered, he found a book on animal motion by J. B. Pettigrew. Wilbur took particular interest in its analysis of flight and the related *Dissertation on Aeronautics*. His imagination was fired by descriptions of how animals as different as birds, fish, reptiles, insects, and mammals were able to fly. Large birds, in particular, could sustain themselves in the air for long periods without any apparent muscular effort. Why, then, should men not find ways to do the same thing?[26]

On May 30 Wilbur wrote to the Smithsonian Institution in Washington, D.C., requesting material on flying and suggestions for further reading. The Smithsonian, a center for aeronautical studies, replied promptly with a packet of four pamphlets, some excerpts from other publications, and a reading list. In June Wilbur began an intensive survey of these and other writings and, within about three months, felt that he knew virtually all that could be gleaned from literature on the subject of aeronautics. He was surprised to find the collection of knowledge to be so small.[27]

He also discovered what he had perhaps known unconsciously all along: that gliding, at its core, was only a necessary intermediate step toward powered flight. What all aeronauts—crackpots as well as serious students—dreamed of was a powered machine that could navigate the sky at the command of its pilot. Far beyond any achievement of gliding as a pastime, a powered machine would generate a revolution in human affairs.

By summer's end, powered flying appeared to Wilbur to involve three elements: an aircraft must have wings designed well enough to lift it into the air, a motor to propel it fast enough to create lift, and a device to control its movements once in the air. The first two of these problems seemed to have been resolved already by Lilienthal and other experimenters. The third appeared to be complicated, but perhaps it was not beyond solution.[28]

The first person to fly a powered airplane would be the one who learned how to maneuver it in the air. That meant controlling the rotation around an imaginary axis connecting the wing tips (pitch), from nose to tail (roll), and, directionally, from side to side (yaw). But the problems could not be solved with slide rules and charts. The solutions depended mainly on learning to control a glider by practicing on one. That done, it should only be necessary to mount an engine on it and take off. (Wilbur's reading also probably introduced him to the view of naturalist John Le Conte, whose article on flying in an 1889 *Popular Science Monthly* concluded that flying machines were "impossible, in spite of the testimony of the birds.")[29]

Gradually Wilbur drew Orville into his studies. Together they found that the status of powered flight at century's end could be summed up very briefly. Thousands of experimenters had tried for centuries to flap themselves into the sky by the strength of their muscles or, more recently, by using motors of one kind or another. But the result had been only to show that these did not seem to be feasible approaches to flying. In 1842 English aeronaut William Henson had conceived the idea of a fixed-wing, steam-powered, propeller-driven airplane as the ultimate solution. Between 1874 and 1894, at least four people had tried unsuccessfully to fly airships of this kind: Du Temple, a Frenchman (1874); Mozhaiski, a Russian (1884); Ader, a Frenchman (1890); and Hiram Maxim, an American (1894).[30]

Maxim's had been a hundred-thousand-dollar, four-ton monstrosity that actually lifted slightly as it sped down a launching ramp, but it achieved nothing more. An inference from his trials—one that few had so far drawn from them—was that power was not the main obstacle to successful flight. If existing motors could lift four tons, they could easily lift smaller, yet entirely serviceable, flying machines. It appears, however, that even Samuel P. Langley of the Smithsonian Institution, one of America's most talented experimenters, had not reached that conclusion.[31]

What a successful flyer must have, Wilbur inferred, was not better machinery so much as better skill. That, in turn, meant practice—far more practice than the five hours or so Lilienthal had spent in the air in five years of experiments.[32]

A Proper Balance

There is little evidence that money was a goal of the Wrights, but wealth would surely be a factor in the race to fly. In 1898 the United States Army (sponsor of Langley's experiments) contracted with him for fifty thousand dollars to build the powered machine he felt he was close to achieving. In May 1896 Langley had sent a steam-powered model with a fourteen-foot wingspan on a flight above the Potomac River. He watched in triumph as his machine climbed majestically in two circles to about one hundred feet. Some ninety seconds after launch, its steam power was exhausted and it wafted down to a smooth landing on the water, having flown over half a mile at speeds up to twenty-five miles an hour. There seemed to be no reason why a larger, slightly improved model should not carry a pilot and respond readily to commands. The Wrights, however, saw that Langley's approach was unlikely to lead to a manned flight: he was taking too lightly the problem of control.[33]

One day in early July 1899, Wilbur was studying some pigeons in flight at the Pinnacles (a small wilderness area outside Dayton) when the answer to controlled flying came to him in a single intuitive flash. It was not so much an observation—pigeon wings moved too fast for that—as a sudden insight that a bird's lateral balance depends on the coordinated movements of its wing tips. Slightly increasing the exposure to the air of the underside of one wing (tilting it upward) increases air pressure beneath the wing and makes it rise. Simultaneous exposure of the topside of the other wing (a downward tilt) increases the pressure above it and causes it to drop, the bird's direction altering to whatever degree it desires. Wilbur realized that what was needed was a machine that could make those adjustments.[34]

Toward the end of July, Wilbur was in the bicycle store toying with a long, slender inner-tube box when the resolution of the problem abruptly presented itself. He found himself idly pressing two corners at one end of the cardboard box and the opposite corners of the other end. The result, he noticed, was to distort the right angles so that an under-surface was exposed at one end; an upper surface mirrored it at the other end. Wilbur immediately envisioned a biplane so constructed that its upper and lower wing tips could be contorted in the same way as the box. Such a plane's wings should duplicate the maneuvers of pigeons. Out of this discovery was born modern aviation.[35]

To test the idea, it would be necessary to construct a model—something on the order of a box kite. Wilbur quickly built a model biplane with upper and lower bamboo wings spanning about five feet. The upper wings, which were cambered like those of Lilienthal, were connected to the lower wings by bamboo struts. (The wings were comparable to opposite broad sides of the inner-tube box.) Hinges at each end of the struts made them flexible enough to twist as the wing tips were altered. (The hinges served the role of the narrow sides of the box.) Flying the model as a kite, it should be possible—by means of hand-held cords—to control the wings as his fingers had controlled the ends of the box. Wilbur and Orville tested the design in August at a field on the edge of town. It flew precisely as Wilbur predicted: they could direct its turns and control its balance.[36] The stage was set for a new era in human travel.

Bill Tate's Siren Song

Gripped by eager anticipation, the Wrights set about designing a full-sized glider embodying the new principle of wing warping. The wings were to be constructed so that the operator, by means of a lever attached to wires, could rotate the wing tips in opposite directions during flight. A so-called elevator was installed at the front of the aircraft. This horizontal rudder should allow the pilot to make the machine climb and descend.[37]

In December 1899 the brothers also wrote to the National Weather Bureau in Washington, stating their purpose and soliciting recommendations for a suitable place to try their experiments. What they required was not a location like Dayton—with its inconstant winds—but a place with steady breezes, sandy soil for soft landings, open space for low-level flying, and one or two good hills for takeoffs. The Weather Bureau recommended sites on both coasts, but it was not until summer that the brothers were ready to make their choice.[38]

In early August 1900, the slack season for the bicycle business having arrived, the Wrights began building a man-carrying model of their design. Seeking more data on a location for "scientific kite flying," Wilbur wrote to the weather station at Kitty Hawk, a remote fishing village on the coastal Outer Banks of eastern North Carolina. His letter of August 3 stated that an ideal location would be one with "a level plain free from trees and shrubbery" and with "a prominent elevation such as a high hill without trees." He also wrote to a station at Myrtle Beach, South Carolina, but got no response.[39]

The chief of the Kitty Hawk weather station, twenty-eight-year-old Joseph J. Dosher, returned a terse reply stating that the beach at Kitty Hawk was about a mile wide, "clear of trees and high hills," and extending sixty miles to the south. The winds in September and October blew mostly from the north and northeast. "I am sorry," he added, "you could not rent a house here, so you will have to bring tents. Hard to obtain board." Perhaps unsure that he had responded adequately, Dosher turned Wilbur's letter over to his neighbor and erstwhile assistant, William James (Bill) Tate—a chap of some education and a way with words—to compose a more complete reply.[40]

Bill Tate, a thirty-year-old native of Kitty Hawk, was—like nearly everyone else living there—a professional fisherman. He was also a Currituck County commissioner and the village's former postmaster. (The post office was now in the name of his wife, Amanda [Addie], but he still conducted most of its business.) Wilbur's letter arrived at an opportune moment, because Tate "had recently been reading up on man's attempts to fly from mythological days to the present and the term 'scientific kite-flying' caught his attention." Thrilled by the idea of being able to watch glider flying from his porch, Tate set about devising a letter on August 18 that would persuade the Wrights to select Kitty Hawk for their experiments.[41] It would be a history-making epistle.

Responding to Wilbur Wright's 1900 request for Outer Banks data, William J. (Bill) Tate wrote him that "our winds are always steady, generally from 10 to 20 miles velocity per hour"—what the Wrights wanted to hear but not a very accurate description of Outer Banks winds. *Courtesy of the Library of Congress, Washington, D.C.*

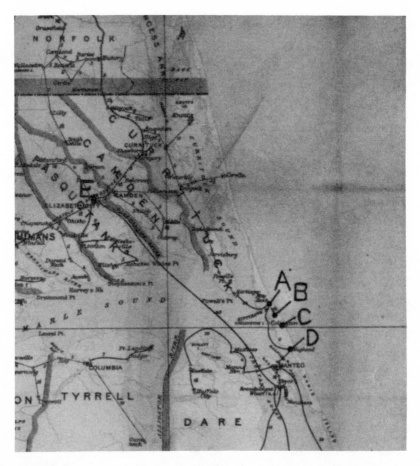

This segment of the 1896 Post Route Map shows the remoteness of Kitty Hawk
(A), Nags Head Woods (B), Kill Devil Hills (C), and Nags Head (D) on the North
Carolina Outer Banks. Kitty Hawk was little more than a fishing village, and transportation between the barrier islands and Elizabeth City (E) was uncertain and
treacherous.

Tate informed the Dayton men that the Kitty Hawk neighborhood,
in his opinion, "would be a fine place" for kite or glider flying. The Wrights
would find there "any type of ground" they wanted. There was, for
example, "a strech of sandy land 1 mile by five with a bare hill in [the]
center 80 feet high not a tree or bush any where to break the evenness of
the wind current." Prevailing winds were "always steady, generally from
10 to 20 miles velocity per hour." Should they require further information
as to Kitty Hawk's topography, he added, R. G. Allen of the Dayton
Weather Bureau had spent a year at Kitty Hawk; he could provide them
with it.[42]

The village of Kitty Hawk, Tate explained, enjoyed a healthy climate. It could be reached by a freight boat from Elizabeth City to the Roanoke Island village of Manteo, twelve miles south of Kitty Hawk, and from there by the Monday-Wednesday-Friday mail boat. There was a telegraph at Kitty Hawk, he informed them. (A telephone line between the Kitty Hawk and Norfolk weather stations may not yet have been in operation.) "You could find [a] good place to pitch tents & get board in private family provided there were not too many in your party." The best time to come would be between mid-September and October 15; waiting later would mean flying in weather that "gets a little rough by November." Tate concluded, "If you decide to try your machine here & come I will take pleasure in doing all I can for your convenience & success & pleasure, & assure you you will find a hospitable people when you come among us."[43]

Tate's letter in some respects overstated the suitability of Kitty Hawk for flying experiments, notably in regard to the "always steady" winds. It also omitted much that the Wrights might need to know in making their plans. He did not tell them, for example, that a vicious hurricane had struck there only the summer before, overwashing the strand from ocean to sound, plowing a temporary inlet through it, and blowing away the wind gauge at Nags Head's lifesaving station after winds reached eighty-five miles an hour.[44]

With the optimum season for winds almost at hand, it may already have been too late for the Wrights to ask for additional information, though Tate's own papers contain a draft letter to them, dated August 26, in which he adds that Kitty Hawk has a half-mile-long strip of sand fifteen hundred yards wide from ocean to bay, with only a few trees at the bay shore. He also mentions nearby Kill Devil Hills, with dunes up to one hundred feet high, sloping gently to their southwest sides. "If," he concludes, "the information given above helps you, or it is the means of bringing you and your brother down in our section I shall feel fully repaid for the little effort on my part in complying with your request." The draft appears, however, to be one Tate composed in later years, trying to duplicate from memory his letter of August 18.[45]

Bill Tate's information was expressed in such an engaging and positive way that it could scarcely be resisted. It was all the invitation Wilbur and Orville needed or could hope for. Rushing their glider to completion, Wilbur was on his way to Kitty Hawk in eighteen days. His "vacation" from the bicycle business was to be an eleven-week sojourn at what would soon seem to him the rim of the world.[46]

CHAPTER THREE

An Outer Banks Adventure

Israel Perry's Washtub

Wilbur Wright, leaving Orville to find someone to mind the store before joining him, departed Dayton on September 6, 1900. With him he carried—besides camping gear—clothes, tools, a large trunk packed with fifty shaped wooden rods, spools of wire, and metal fittings, and French sateen wing coverings. This was the glider minus some eighteen-foot wing spars, which he intended to purchase en route. He rode the Chesapeake and Ohio Railroad to Old Point Comfort in southeastern Virginia, arriving in the early evening of the next day. A steamer ferry took him across Hampton Roads to Norfolk and a night's rest at the Monticello Hotel.[1]

The next day was spent in a futile search of local mills for eighteen-foot spruce spars. Finding none that long available, he settled for sixteen-foot spars of white pine, which would mean smaller wings and require that his fitted cloth coverings be resewn once he reached Kitty Hawk. (The total outlay for glider parts was about fifteen dollars.) In late afternoon he caught a train to Elizabeth City, checking in that evening at M. J. Sawyer's Arlington Hotel. After a night's rest, he set out to arrange boat passage for himself and his baggage to Kitty Hawk, a trip of about fifteen miles downriver to Albemarle Sound and perhaps twenty-five miles across to Kitty Hawk's wharf, on the sound side.[2]

Bill Tate's letter had led Wilbur to suppose he would have no trouble finding a boat headed in that direction. Instead, he found to his dismay that the first people he talked to had never heard of Kitty Hawk; obviously, they had no idea how to get there. This was Wilbur's first encounter with Outer Banks isolation. (He had missed by a day the weekly freight boat to Manteo, Bill Tate's recommended route.) Finally, on September 11, he located Israel Perry, a loquacious Colington Island fisherman and Kitty Hawk native who owned—and lived aboard—a small, flat-bottomed schooner. Perry agreed to transport Wright and his gear for three dollars.[3] It sounded like a bargain.

Arriving at the wharf, Wilbur learned that the schooner was anchored three miles downriver and could be reached only in Perry's leaky skiff. Wondering aloud if the skiff was safe, he was offered reassurance: "Oh," said Perry, "It's safer than the *big* boat." The trip downriver was an ordeal of rowing and bailing in a boat loaded to capacity. And the mother vessel proved, indeed, to be sorrier than its leaky offspring. As Wilbur helped Perry and the cabin boy transfer his baggage to the *Curlicue*, he noted that the schooner's rudderpost was nearly rotted off, its cabin dirty and full of vermin, its sails rotten. But the afternoon sky was clear and a light wind from the north gave promise of a smooth passage to Kitty Hawk.[4] Wilbur could not guess that he was about to be introduced to the meteorological cussedness of the Outer Banks.

Perry, his creaking sailboat transformed into the world's first aircraft carrier, weighed anchor shortly after dinner. (Wilbur declined to partake of the captain's noisome fare.) The wind was so light that it took hours to clear the river and head into Albemarle Sound. Surprisingly, the water turned rough despite the gentle breeze; as night fell, the wind began increasing and shifting to the southeast. The schooner responded badly to the demand of sailing into the wind; heavy waves began pushing the *Curlicue* northeastward. Rolling and pitching, the schooner began to leak and waves broke over its bow. By 11:00 P.M. the wind was a gale and the foresail, "with a terrible roar," snapped loose from its boom. The wind's force was now such that to turn back would risk being swamped.[5]

To get out of rough water and avoid shipwreck, Perry struggled to put his boat into the mouth of North River (the next stream east of the Pasquotank). This was made more dangerous by the mainsail's breaking loose at the bottom, leaving only the jib functional. It required, in addition, that the boat be allowed to swing around in inky darkness with its stern into the wind. While waves broke heavily over the stern, Perry somehow steered the schooner to safety in the narrow upper part of the river.[6]

Wilbur, thoroughly soaked, had been fully employed with the cabin boy during most of the evening bailing water and taking in ripped sails. Perry would not hear of going ashore for the night owing to the "bars" that he claimed inhabited the woods.[7] This was a fearful introduction to the hazards of the region where Wilbur meant to sail the skies in a glider made of sticks and rags.

The next day was mercifully calm, allowing for morning repairs to the *Curlicue*'s sails and an easy late afternoon trip to Kitty Hawk. The village, however, came into sight only at nightfall, its wharf and adjacent store shut down and unlighted; so Wilbur had to spend another night aboard the docked boat. Spurning Perry's reeking kitchen during the entire voyage, Wilbur had subsisted on a jar of jelly packed for him by his sister.[8]

Next morning, September 13, he finally got ashore with his baggage. Since leaving Dayton, Wilbur had covered seven hundred miles in the first day and a half, but only forty in the past four and a half. Israel Perry, nonetheless, had performed what he was hired to do: Wilbur and his gear were delivered to his destination undamaged. If, as Orville later claimed, Wilbur's adventure "rescued the name of Israel Perry . . . from oblivion" at Kitty Hawk, it was an honor the old salt had earned. Unfortunately, Perry appears to have been forced out of business soon by unfavorable publicity generated by this voyage.[9]

The House of Tate

A smallish fourteen-year-old, Elijah William Baum (son of George W. and Matilda Etheridge Baum, whose home was at the head of Kitty Hawk Bay), happened to be at the wharf when Wilbur arrived. The lad agreed to guide him to Bill Tate's home, about a quarter of a mile from the wharf. Responding to a knock at his door around nine o'clock in the morning, Tate found Elijah and, he later wrote, "a strange gentleman." He "took off his cap and introduced himself as Wilbur Wright of Dayton, Ohio, 'to whom you wrote concerning this section.'"[10]

Having received no response to his letter of August 18, Tate was not expecting him; but, without hesitation, he invited him in. Wilbur, as Tate afterward recalled, was "asked to be seated and we began a conversation." The visitor related his harrowing adventure aboard Israel Perry's schooner, "how the miserable little boat," as Tate remembered it, "had to run for harbor in a blow and how he could not eat the provender cooked by the two men on the boat, and how consequently he had been without food for 48 hours."[11]

Bill Tate had heard as much from many another who had tried crossing the sound in small craft; he found hilarious Wilbur's "graphic description of the rolling of the boat," which left "his back . . . sore from lying on the deck" and "the muscles of his arms aching from holding on when the boat rolled." (This wasn't insensitivity on Tate's part; Wilbur sent home a comic narrative of the voyage that the family quoted for years.)[12]

His host recognized that Wilbur's first need now was for nourishment. "It being the breakfast hour, about 9:30 a. m.," Tate later recalled, "a hasty fire was made in the kitchen stove. Mrs. Tate got busy; the aroma of ham and eggs was soon permeating the house, a meal was soon ready, Mr. Wright seated himself and done a he-man's part by that humble

Wilbur Wright was a guest at the William J. Tate home during his first three weeks at Kitty Hawk in the autumn of 1900; Orville, arriving later, spent six nights there before the Wrights set up their camp nearby. The first Wright glider was constructed in the front yard. The house, built by Tate about 1897, served as the village post office in 1900 and as a Methodist parsonage before it burned. *Courtesy of Daniel Grady Tate.*

breakfast." They also made terms for Wilbur's board and lodging. (This included providing a pitcher of boiled water each morning from the shallow eighteen-foot surface well in the yard—a defense against typhoid—until he could set up his camp.) In addition, it was arranged that Orville might share Wilbur's room when he arrived.[13]

Addie Tate, however, harbored some misgivings about the arrangement on the ground that her fare and accommodations might be too plain for a city man. But Wilbur, overhearing a discussion of this between Addie and Bill, offered them reassurance: "Mrs. Tate," he interposed, "we shall be guests in your house; your fare will be our fare." The grateful Tates, convinced that their boarder was a gentleman of breeding, would never forget that the Wrights were "sons of a bishop and had been brought up in the Christian way of life."[14]

Despite an exhausting journey, Wilbur was ready for work the next morning. Bill Tate took him in a horse cart to fetch his gear from the wharf and accompanied him to Kitty Hawk's lifesaving station to introduce him to the crew. They also visited the wharf again on September 17, when the triweekly mail boat arrived with the pine spars and other material Wilbur had stored at Elizabeth City.[15]

Shown here in 1900 are Bill Tate, his wife Amanda (Addie), and daughters Irene and Pauline, aged three and two respectively. The young woman standing is Miss Nancy Baum, a friend and nearby neighbor of the Tates. *Photograph by the Wright brothers from Wright State University, Dayton, Ohio.*

On the latter day Wilbur set up a canvas lean-to and started assembling his glider in Tate's yard, "between the porch and the road." Decades later, older inhabitants still recalled seeing him in the weeks that followed "down on his knees in the yard at work while his materials were kept handy on the porch." On or about the fourteenth, his second day at Tate's, he got off a letter to his anxious Dayton kin, no doubt recounting in florid detail his voyage with Israel Perry. They could rest assured, however, that the Kitty Hawkers were "friendly and neighborly." All was going well.[16]

Within a week or so, Wilbur had had an opportunity to take stock of his new surroundings and form an idea of what life had in store for him and Orville in the next couple of months. The frame, T-shaped Tate home, one of Kitty Hawk's most substantial, was typical (except for its large rear portion) of the favored local type: two stories, one room deep, with a breezeway. The siding, neither planed nor painted, bore the runic record of savage hurricanes and "nor'easters" that frequently battered the Outer Banks. The house was innocent of such Dayton amenities as carpets on its floors, plaster on its walls, books, or pictures; there was also "very little

furniture." But its hospitality was genuine and the circumstances condu-
cive to the sort of work the Wrights must do there.[17]

Bill Tate was an up-and-coming young man, a local leader as
Currituck County commissioner and notary public; his livelihood was
gleaned largely from commercial fishing. His mother died in 1877 when
he was eight; in 1880 his father froze to death when his boat overturned
in Currituck Sound. Better educated than most of his neighbors, Bill had
attended school for four years (1882-1886) at Oxford Masonic Orphan-
age in the North Carolina Piedmont and graduated from Atlantic Colle-
giate Institute in Elizabeth City. After returning to Kitty Hawk, he worked
in his uncle Daniel's store and took it over at Daniel's death. When the
store burned not long afterward, he built a new house with living quarters,
post office, and store combined. It was there that the Wright brothers
stayed in 1900. Bill, a constant reader and apt conversationalist, took an
immediate liking for Wilbur. He would remain close to the Wright family
for the next half century and more.[18]

The Tates' two children, daughters Irene and Pauline (Lena), were
three and two respectively. Their first son, Elijah William, was born that
winter. Lewis came two years later. Don Quixote, Bill's venerable horse,
regarded as the patriarch of local horseflesh, rounded out the family. Bill's
thirty-nine-year-old half brother Daniel (Dan), Daniel's wife, Palestine
Basnight Tate, and their six children lived close by.[19]

The Kitty Hawk Tates were the progeny of William D. Tate, the son
of immigrant Scots and a native of Maine. In 1848 Bill and Dan's father
was first mate on the sailing ship *Dreadmanfort* when it made a trans-
atlantic crossing in fourteen days—a record that remained intact until it
was broken half a century later by a steamship. In March 1849, when
William was twenty-four, he was the master of the clipper ship *B. M.
Prescott*, en route from Boston to California with gold prospectors, when
the vessel was blown aground near Kitty Hawk. He and his brother Daniel,
the first mate, were rescued by a group of Kitty Hawk residents led by
Elijah Sibbern (whose daughter, Addie, Bill Tate married), and both
decided to settle there. Many Outer Banks families, in fact, could trace
their origins to refugees from shipwrecks.[20]

Like the Tates, Kitty Hawkers in general were a tough, resilient, and
self-reliant lot—although they shared little of the Wrights' disciplined
work ethic. (One of them later recalled that Wilbur at Kill Devil Hills told
his hired carpenter that "a nail dropped was not worth the time it took to
pick it up.") Some had regular employment at a pair of United States
Lifesaving Service stations: one a mile north of Kitty Hawk, with the
weather station alongside; the other four miles south of the village, near
a desert site called Kill Devil Hills.[21]

The People of the Banks

Though generally of scant means, the "Bankers" were rarely in real want, thanks to the bounty of the sea, sky, and forests. The soil, mostly fine sand, was dotted, especially on the western or Albemarle Sound side, by numerous small patches of richer ground, allowing nearly every family a garden with corn, beans, turnips, potatoes, beets, watermelons, and such. They also raised chickens, some cattle and hogs (made scrawny by inadequate forage), and sheep (kept mainly for the wool). In addition, every family was likely to have a few apple, pear, and peach trees. Produce not consumed fresh was either canned or traded at Elizabeth City and elsewhere for other goods. "Their success is not great," Wilbur wrote home, "but it is a wonder that they can raise anything at all."[22]

By a wide margin, the main business of Bankers was commercial fishing, much of it done in the sounds using small boats and long nets. The supply of seafood could be counted on even following the most destructive storms. Fishermen turned out for spring runs of shad and herring, when vast, glistening schools flooded through the inlets to spawn in the brackish sounds or freshwater rivers of the mainland. Other fishing seasons followed in summer and fall, when boats with three- or four-man crews made their way to the ocean through Oregon and other inlets. A brief oyster-dredging season in December provided local residents with Christmas money.[23]

In a good year, profits from fishing could be substantial. Outer Banks shad and sturgeon roe enjoyed a brisk sale in northern markets, as did oysters—the Chesapeake Bay's great beds having been depleted in the nineteenth century. The fishermen also took menhaden (for fertilizer), rock bass, croaker, bluefish, and spot. These were boated to the mainland for sale to dealers and others or bartered for corn and other goods; any left over were salted for winter use.[24]

There was also plenty of game, including squirrel and bear, in nearby woods. Wilbur described the Kitty Hawkers as "game hogs" who, with scant regard for legal seasons and limits, hunted when and where they pleased. In particular, there were innumerable birds: eagles, ospreys, fish and hen hawks, sea gulls, and migratory geese and ducks. Wildfowl feeding grounds along Albemarle and Currituck sounds enticed droves of hunters from distant places each year. Bankers often served as guides.[25]

Some Bankers even hunted wildfowl commercially, shipping the flesh to northern markets, where it was in high demand. Former colonies of egrets and herons were all but extinct by then, having been sacrificed to the vagaries of feathered fashion in northern cities. When not fishing, a Banker usually headed for the woods in early morning to hunt. Morris and Edward A. Beal were among the local men whose primary occupation was recorded by the 1900 census taker as that of "wildfowl huntsmen."[26]

The lifesaving crews, known as surfmen, were local residents of nearby communities, such as the Roanoke Island town of Manteo. Those with families might occupy one or the other of several small houses near their stations. The rest resided in the station house and went home perhaps once a week and on two-month summer vacations. The main responsibility of surfmen was to patrol the beaches, watching for ships dangerously near shore and warning them away with flares. When ships ran aground too far out for rescue lines to be fired over them, the work could become extremely dangerous. Then surfmen would take to open boats, battling waves and wind, to reach survivors. The stations, later absorbed into the Coast Guard, were scattered at intervals of seven miles or so along the Outer Banks.[27]

Wilbur found the people to be as friendly as Bill Tate had promised, but there was enough reserve on both sides to smother—in most cases— any chance of genuine intimacy. From the standpoint of Mrs. Adam D. (Lillie) Etheridge of Kitty Hawk, the Wrights "were nice looking men, but they didn't have much to do with people. They just stayed in their camp and kept to themselves and would only go down to the Station to collect their mail. I never saw them go inside; they would just go to the door, and someone would take their mail out to them. It wasn't that they didn't like people, they were just very secretive about what they were doing." Still, "[t]hey talked to us," another resident would recall, "about the things they thought we were interested in and anyone with a doubt in his mind about anything could always get the sympathetic ear of the Wrights."[28]

The hamlet of Kitty Hawk, then in Currituck County, consisted of two settlements with an open area between. The northwest section was known as "up the road"; the southeast, "down the road." Actually, the community was little more than a secluded fish camp, with about sixty houses scattered among the marshes and woods fronting the sound. One or two of the houses functioned as stores.[29]

Dr. John L. Cogswell, a forty-five-year-old Connecticut native who was married to Addie Tate's sister Maxine, attended to local health problems. Young Tom Tate (son of Dan) owed his life to Dr. Cogswell, who had taken him into his home to nurse him through an ordeal of scarlet fever followed by pneumonia. On one occasion, Tom boasted to the Wrights that Dr. Cogswell was reckoned to be the community's richest man, a judgment grounded in a report that the doctor's brother owed him fifteen thousand dollars![30]

Kitty Hawk had two churches, a parsonage, and an ungraded school with one teacher, twenty-five-year-old Joseph Cahoon. The Nags Head

Woods community also had a Baptist church and a school. Virtually all permanent residents lived on the sound side of the peninsula. They had learned not to build homes among the dunes because sand sooner or later buried everything in its wind-driven migrations. For about five miles to the south the only break in the barren landscape was a cluster of dunes called Kill Devil Hills. (The lush growth found there today is largely a result of New Deal land-reclamation programs.)[31]

Kitty Hawk Bay and village, 1900. The Wright brothers made this picture from their first campsite just southeast of the village, which consisted of only a handful of frame houses, a Methodist church, a small school, and one or two stores. *Library of Congress.*

Kitty Hawk at close quarters probably seemed more isolated to Wilbur Wright than it really was. Nine miles south lay Nags Head village, a popular summer resort. In late June of each year, steamers and sailboats began bringing hundreds of visitors to cavort for a day, spend short vacations, or remain for the summer. Overnight accommodations were available at ocean- or sound-side cottages and at John Z. Lowe's Hotel, with its one hundred rooms, large covered porches, dining hall, well-attended bar, pavilion, and tenpin alley. During the summer Nags Head enjoyed daily steamboat connections with Elizabeth City and other mainland towns, plus frequent visits by excursion steamers.[32]

The welfare of the whole peninsula was affected by Nags Head's summer business. The livelihood of Mrs. Solomon (Mary) Moore of Nags Head Woods, for example, came chiefly from fortune-telling for vacationers. The Herbert and Tilghman Tillett families, the Baums, and the Perrys—farmers at or near Kitty Hawk—were among those who supplied the sound-side hotel and restaurants with regular cartloads of fresh vegetables. But nearly all the vacationers had returned home, and the restaurants and hotel closed for the season, by the time Wilbur arrived in mid-September.[33]

The weeks here would be too few, the days too demanding, to allow the Wright brothers to visit Nags Head or delve into the region's colorful past. Scattered along the beaches lay stark skeletons of some of the hundreds of wrecked vessels, the scavenging of which first lured settlers here in the eighteenth century. Not a few families decorated their homes with the weather-beaten figureheads and other relics of shipwrecks.

Here sixteenth-century Spanish explorers had landed, Blackbeard and generations of pirates had caroused, Confederate and Yankee armies camped. A few miles south, on Roanoke Island, lay the sand- and vine-covered remains of the first two English settlements in America. Frequently the shifting sands unveiled the sites of Indian villages and burying grounds that had once honeycombed the region.[34] None of this is more than hinted at, however, in the voluminous records the Wrights kept of their visits on this or subsequent occasions.

Of Gasoline and Wild Goose

Unaccustomed to the hot southern sun, Wilbur Wright found his work of assembling the glider in Tate's yard to be especially demanding. He needed to test and retest each part as he fitted it, lest some preventable accident befall the project. Although Bill Tate hovered constantly about, he could be of no help in this highly technical procedure. The fifty-two-pound aircraft would be required to carry aloft up to five times its weight; the workmanship would be sternly challenged. The lives of both brothers depended on painstaking attention to every detail.[35]

By September 23 Wilbur could boast in a letter to his Dayton kin that "I have my machine nearly finished." Before the wings could be completed, it was necessary to resew their cloth coverings to match the smaller spars and reduced dimensions he had been forced to accept at Norfolk. Fortunately, Addie Tate owned a pedal-operated Kenwood sewing machine. She graciously let it be set up on the front porch, where she assisted Wilbur in making the alterations.[36]

Orville arrived at the Kitty Hawk wharf on September 28, loaded down with a big tent, his personal belongings, and supplies of goods all but unobtainable at Kitty Hawk: sugar, coffee, and other foodstuffs. The Tates moved him into Wilbur's room; and, within a couple of days, the Wrights finished the glider by attaching the lower wing and elevator. On October 4 the brothers moved from the Tates' house into the campsite they had selected at Lookout Hill, half a mile east, which covered the remains of an old house. Thereafter Orville, who had some talent for cooking, prepared the meals; Wilbur washed the dishes.[37]

Kitty Hawkers eyed the brothers curiously from their windows and boats, trying to understand why grown men would behave the way they did. But the attention was kindly, and the Wrights earned a measure of respect early by tending strictly to their own business. In Bill Tate's eyes, the newcomers "were frugal but lived well. I knew for I . . . lunched with them at their tent often." There appeared to be nothing really needful lacking at their primitive quarters except, perhaps, a privy such as those that stood behind every Kitty Hawk house. Tate, for one, felt that none was necessary at the camp since "it was only a few yards to the thick copse of bushy undergrowth and hardly any one ever passed that way."[38]

The finished glider, a thing of riveting fascination to Bill Tate and his neighbors, was a tailless biplane with a rudder, or elevator (horizontal slats for ascending and descending), thrusting out thirty inches in front of the wings. As in Wilbur's model of the previous summer, the wings were made so that the operator—lying on his stomach at the middle of the lower wing—could, with a lever at his side, twist the wing tips, simultaneously exposing alternate surfaces to the winds as in the cardboard-box experiment. This procedure came to be called wing-warping.[39]

Throughout this and later phases of the fall work the pair was joined daily by Bill Tate, who took an interest in everything they did and was no doubt highly pleased with himself for having had a part in bringing such an entertaining project to Kitty Hawk. He was sent by the brothers in their first days together to Elizabeth City to buy some tin dishes, a three-burner stove and small oven, and a barrel of gasoline. Bill, who had never seen gasoline before, procured some at N. G. Grandy and Company but was uncertain how to handle it and not a little alarmed by it. "I never will forget," he later wrote, "that I wrapped it in a tarpaulin & put it way up forward in the boat so it would be as far from me . . . as possible. I was afraid of it but I took the wrong precaution. I should have left it out in the open." He arrived home safely, however, with his fearsome burden. Apparently these were the first gasoline and first oilstove ever brought to Kitty Hawk.[40]

The Wrights, for their part, were delighted to have a local man so caught up in their project. "Tate can't afford to shirk his [own] work," Orville wrote home, "to fool around with us, so he attempts to do a day's work in two or three hours so that he can spend the balance with us and the machine." He "gets interested in anything we have," noted Orville, "wants to put acetylene gas in his house because he saw my bicycle gas lamp, has decided to buy our gasoline stove when we leave."[41] In Bill Tate the Wright brothers had discovered a kindred spirit.

Tate and the Wrights gradually learned that they shared other tastes besides flying. In early October Bill invited the brothers home for a midday meal of wild goose, one of five that a neighbor, "old man Baum," had killed out of season. Tate bought it for fifty cents, already dressed, and Addie added "all the trimmings." Learning that the Wrights had never tasted wild goose, Bill politely warned his guests that it "had a wild gamey flavor that some people did not like. . . . We all sailed in," he wrote afterward, "and it was not long before Wilbur asked 'Please pass the platter of goose. I want some more of that wild gamey flavor.'" Orville allowed in a letter home that the goose "tasted pretty good after a fast of several weeks in any kind of flesh except a mess or two of fish."[42]

"Belly Bumpums" from Lookout Hill

On a level stretch of sand at their camp, the Wrights erected a simple, fifteen-foot wooden tower, or derrick. Since the glider was expected to carry a man, it was tethered from the tower by a rope to prevent it from soaring to dangerous heights in sudden gusts. Neither of the brothers was willing to run unnecessary risks of accidents that might end their experiments prematurely. If things went well with the glider restricted in this way, they could try free flying later on. Weatherman Joe Dosher lent them his hand-held wind gauge to measure the speed of the winds before each flight, a critical factor.[43]

Since all their time in the air during these weeks was likely to amount to only a few minutes, it was agreed that Wilbur would do all the flying. In this way, he hoped to gain a comfortable command over the machine and thus be an expert teacher when Orville began learning. But, as it turned out, all the flying for the 1900 season was performed on just six days between October 3 and 19.[44]

After several unmanned flights, apparently on the morning of October 3, Wilbur let impatience get the better of him: he decided to risk a trial of riding the glider off the slope of Lookout Hill. With Orville and Tate holding fifteen-to-twenty-foot ropes attached to each wing, he lay facedown on the lower wing ("belly bumpums," a Kitty Hawker called it). He was some fifteen feet in the air when he found that inexperience prevented him from holding the machine steady. Wilbur, shouting for his handlers to bring him down, resolved to content himself for the time being with unmanned test flights.[45]

There were more trials that afternoon and again on the ninth, sometimes with the tethered glider empty and sometimes carrying a load of chains of various weights borrowed from Bill Tate. Further flights followed on October 10 but ended abruptly when the unattended glider was suddenly caught by a wind gust, tossed into the air, and slammed down with a sickening crunch. Three precious days were consumed in repairing the mess.[46] In the event of a return to Kitty Hawk, a hangar would be vital to the mission.

Disappointingly, the trials showed that the weighted glider, with the smaller, rebuilt wings, could not be sustained in flight with winds of less than twenty-five miles an hour or flown at all in winds much higher than that. Instead of the consistent fifteen-mile-an-hour winds the brothers rather naïvely expected, the Outer Banks—while averaging about that—might be totally calm one day and swept by a sixty-mile-an-hour blow the next. This meant that many days were unsuitable for any flying, greatly limiting opportunities for trials. There were also frequent time-consuming trips to the Tates' for water for drinking, cooking, and bathing.[47] If the Wrights returned in a later season, a camp well would be a high priority.

Tom Tate, Nineteenth-Century Aeronaut

By now the Wrights were well known around Kitty Hawk. "Every place we go," Orville wrote his sister, "we are called Mr. Wright." Bill Tate, given his closer association with them, seems to have become comfortable with the respectful and friendly forms "Mr. Wilbur" and "Mr. Orville." Following a heavy storm on the night of October 9, Orville wrote home that "the Kitty Hawkers were out early peering around the edge of the woods and out of their upstairs windows to see whether our camp was still in existence."[48] But the onlookers had other interests as well, including the novel spectacle of the glider mens' manic discipline.

Years later surfman John T. Daniels recalled: "I never saw two men so wrapped up in their work in my life. They had their whole heart and soul in what they were doing, and when they were working we could come around and stand right over them and they wouldn't pay any more attention to us than if we weren't there at all. After their day's work was over they were different; then they were the nicest fellows you ever saw and treated us fine." Daniels and his close friend Adam Dough Etheridge (they were married to half sisters) were to become frequent visitors to the Wright camp.[49]

The Wrights' presence soon upset the delicately balanced village economy. Their demand for eggs had, by mid-October, exhausted "the output of all the henneries within a mile" of their camp. Having also bought nearly all the canned goods off the skimpy shelves of Jesse A. Cahoon, the village storekeeper, Orville feared that some of the residents might "have to suffer as a result." Cahoon, sixty-two years old and in poor health, was the schoolmaster's father. He had come from the mainland in the hope of recovery but revealed mournfully to Orville that it was the "greatest mistake" of his life; that he would "die here before I can get away." (In fact, he did not die there but gave up the store in early October, selling his remaining stock and leaving Kitty Hawk.)[50]

By mid-October the kite and gliding experiments were attracting considerable attention. Neighborhood boys watched the activities when they could and were sometimes even asked to participate. "They would get some of us boys," recalled Joseph B. Weisiger of Manteo, "to take a kite and hold it up . . . while they manipulated its four strings. We'd get mad when they'd pull the kite down just when it got to sailing best."[51]

On October 17 Dan Tate and his son Tom, a self-assured eleven-year-old ("Tom the fisherman" the Wrights called him in tribute to his piscatorial prowess), came over to ogle and help out. The machine was flown several times as a kite with Tom aboard, his seventy pounds less of a burden on the glider than Wilbur's larger frame. Thus Tom, unheralded for it to this day, became the first Tar Heel to fly a true glider. This event took place a good nine months before Orville's first glider flight. (Tom, it will be observed, flew in the nineteenth century, Orville only in the twentieth!)[52]

Because they planned to leave for Dayton on October 23 and could not rely on the winds before that time, the Wrights decided to risk at least one free flight on the afternoon of the seventeenth. With the help of Dan and Tom Tate, they carried the machine three miles south to Kill Devil Hill, a dune about a hundred feet high—the tallest of the three known collectively as Kill Devil Hills.[53]

After the glider was placed on the dune's southwestern slope, Wilbur got in it, with Orville and Dan each holding a wing tip. Simply lifting the glider off the ground by hand did not work, so Orville and Tate tried running down the slope, each holding a wing, before releasing it. (Wilbur ran too, jumping into place at the last instant.) This resulted in a splendid flight of about sixty feet and a smooth landing. About a dozen short flights were made during the day, and the results bolstered the Wrights' confidence that most of their ideas were sound.[54]

The final flights of the season came on October 18 and 19, the Wrights at first tossing the unmanned glider from the dunes to see what it would do. The machine would climb to a height of fifteen or twenty feet for a short distance and then drop, sometimes hitting the slope of the dune with a dull thud. This generally meant a broken strut or wire and hasty repairs before the next launch. Eventually, Wilbur elected to mount

Thomas Douglas (Tom) Tate (1888-1956), twelve years old when the Wrights captured him on film in 1901, posed before their glider. Noted for his fishing prowess, Tom displayed his latest catch, a big drum. A frequent visitor to the camp of the Wrights, who called him "Tom the fisherman," he was a son of Daniel M. Tate, Bill Tate's half brother. *Library of Congress.*

the machine again and was thrilled when the last of his several flights went for distances of up to four hundred feet and for as long as fifteen seconds. He found that he could land safely and precisely; his gliding experience had begun to pay off.[55]

There remained stubborn problems to resolve during the winter, but the Wrights (and their friend Bill Tate) were by now totally obsessed with the art of gliding. It seemed clear that their initial machine was the best glider ever built. Perhaps the remaining problems could be worked out over the following months; then they could come back the next year with a better machine and more sophisticated techniques. In any event, the sea air and outdoor activity had been a tonic for the northerners, and they were well pleased with their oceanside vacation.

The glider had served its purpose by showing how a better one could be made, so there was no need to spend time taking the now-rickety machine apart and hauling it back to Dayton. Just before departing from Kitty Hawk on the twenty-third in Israel Perry's boat, the Wrights carried the glider to the top of a dune and hurled it downhill. The wrecked aircraft came to rest in a hollow, where the brothers shoveled some sand on it to keep it from blowing about.[56]

Although Bill Tate regretted the end of the flying season, it was probably fortunate for him that the Wrights did not stay longer. The fall fishing season, a primary source of his livelihood, had begun in early October and he was already in danger of losing a significant part of his annual income. Moreover, Dr. Cogswell told Orville only half jokingly that he feared Tate would "be dead before Christmas from excitement if [you] don't get out."[57]

Agent Bill Tate

In Bill Tate, the Wrights gained a devoted friend and partisan for the rest of their lives. At the end of their 1900 vacation, the brothers sold him their gasoline stove for three dollars—though there seemed little prospect that he would overcome his fear of the thing and use it. They also told him he was welcome to the wreckage of the glider and any scraps of lumber and whatnot left lying about the camp. But they enjoined him strictly not to divulge the machine's dimensions to inquiring parties or allow pictures to be made of it.[58]

With no guarantee that the brothers would return in 1901 for more flying, Tate was anxious to keep alive the prospect; he wrote them in early November to ensure that the relationship would remain close. He could reveal, no doubt to their chagrin, that Kitty Hawk's weather had reverted to Indian summer. "On the day you departed," he wrote, "a specially fine spell seemed to set in & it is lasting yet." Perhaps owing to the fine weather, he and other fishermen were taking plenty of "nice ocean fish," and "northern market prices" were good.[59] His income would be gratifying in spite of the days given over to flying.

Tate had lately visited the Wright camp, in company with his neighbor Walter W. Best, and examined the wrecked glider, finding a quarter ton of sand on its wings. They removed the sand, put the wreck in his cart, and brought it home, where he took it apart. Finding it "builded better than I expected," he saved its ash ribs for "a special purpose." He also

William James (Bill) Tate (1869-1953). Tate was the Wright brothers' first host at Kitty Hawk, a vital aid in their early trips there, and a lifelong champion of them and their work. Tate's letter in the summer of 1900 was a principal cause of their selecting the Outer Banks for their experiments. *Courtesy of Daniel Grady Tate, Bill's grandnephew.*

claimed to have done some cooking on the gasoline stove, finding that "it works capital." Addie joined him in best wishes "& sincerely hoping we may someday meet again."[60]

The Wrights might well have been astonished to learn what became of the wrecked glider. (Prized remnants yet remain in the hands of Banker descendants and others, though it is impossible to say which of several wrecked machines any of them came from.) Parts of the machine were given away and small pieces were used by Dan Tate's children—evidently Tom, his six-year-old sister Fidelia, and possibly their brother Edward, an eighteen-year-old sailor, to build a kite. The kite was said to have been made large enough to carry one of them, but fortunately it broke before being put to the test.[61]

Having the scraps dumped in her yard, Addie Tate examined the sateen wing coverings and discovered that they were of a quality unobtainable on the Banks. She cut away the cloth, pulled out the staples,

removed some rust spots, and washed it. Then she used portions of the
material to make dresses for her daughters, Irene and Lena, and gave the
rest away. Wilbur found the girls still wearing the sateen garments in 1901.
In Lena's recollection, hers was "an ordinary little dress, with a sash that
tied behind in a bow, but my Mother was handy with a needle and she
insisted that our clothes look pretty." Neighbors were said to have used
their portions to make blouses for their sons, baby clothes, and handker-
chiefs, among other things.[62]

In addition, it was said that some scrap lumber from the Wright camp
was used by Bill Tate to help construct a barn, though the material may
well have come from an old house he tore down near the camp in October
to keep sand from burying it. Apparently the remaining scraps were used
for firewood during the winter.[63] In any event, nothing that was usable
was left to rot. Over years of salvaging gifts from the tides, Bankers had
learned that the wise exploitation of debris could mean the difference
between a good year and a bad one. (As will be seen, scraps of flying-ma-
chine material now represented as coming from a Wright flying machine
may have come from any of seven machines, three of them built by persons
other than the Wrights.)

All in all, and despite some time wasted by the menfolk in fooling
around with kites and strings, Kitty Hawkers could look back on their
experience with the Ohioans as a welcome break from the harsh demands
of daily existence. The visitors had been self-sufficient men who, although
glad for whatever help they received, made no demands on their hosts and
neighbors. They were unfailingly courteous and—somewhat surprisingly—dressed even on the hottest or wettest days in a manner the Bankers
reserved for Sundays. The sight of their graceful machine soaring above
the dunes was one that no witness would ever forget.

As the Wrights entered the Bankers' folklore, they were also credited
with being "very nice to children, and," commented Lena Tate, they "had
been brought up in a Christian way of life. When they came to our house
they were very considerate of Mother, carried up their own washing water
and did everything for themselves. . . . Wilbur was more outgoing than
Orville. I believe that Wilbur was the sharper of the two, he was the leading
spirit of the team; he led and Orville followed."[64] This was a shrewd
observation of a unique relationship.

An unexpected bonus of the Wrights' Kitty Hawk sojourn had been
the interest and cooperation of the Outer Bankers. Most of the services
performed for the brothers were done voluntarily. The use of Addie Tate's
sewing machine and Joe Dosher's anemometer, the stimulus of Bill Tate's
enthusiasm, Tom Tate's willingness to be borne aloft on a stick-and-cloth
glider—all contributed to the Wrights' experiments and advanced the
cause of aviation. It was, therefore, not only the essential combination of

wind and sand that made Kitty Hawk important to the airplane project: the wholehearted hospitality and assistance of the natives made the choice of location fortuitous.

CHAPTER FOUR

The Trials at Kill Devil Hill

The Omen

Reflecting during the winter on their experience at Kitty Hawk, the Wrights had reason to be pleased with what they had achieved there. They had proved to themselves the importance of wing warping to control roll and the effectiveness of the front elevator for regulating nose-to-tail movement (pitch). Their total time in the air had been only a few minutes, but it was enough to demonstrate that they could fly their glider with a fair measure of control and—provided they kept close to the ground—little danger of serious injury. Both were satisfied that they were on the right track toward a motor-driven machine in the near future.

Wilbur and Orville soon set to work designing a new and larger glider for 1901. By using larger wings with increased camber, they planned to have a machine weighing ninety-eight pounds, almost double the weight of the 1900 version. It would, in fact, be a much larger glider than anyone had ever tried to fly before.[1]

In May they wrote to Octave Chanute, an eminent Chicago engineer and glider enthusiast whom they had known for about a year, informing him that they would probably spend another six or eight weeks on the Outer Banks early in the fall. They agreed to Chanute's request to pay them a brief visit there and—somewhat reluctantly—to accept the services of two people he proposed to have join them.[2]

One of these helpers was a young Pennsylvanian, George A. Spratt, an aeronautics buff and medical college graduate (though he no longer practiced medicine). His presence could be especially useful in the event of an accident or illness. The other, Tennessean E. C. Huffaker, was building a glider for Chanute. It was suggested that he might test his glider there as well as offer useful assistance to the Wrights. Self-sufficient in their work and mistrustful of the motives and technical acumen of the intruders, the Wrights accepted all this only to gratify Chanute, whose encouragement they valued.[3]

In June 1901 the brothers began to get national and even international attention for their studies and experiments in flight. Chanute that month published a journal article on aeronautics in which he made brief reference to their work. In July Wilbur published a pair of technical articles in American and German aeronautical journals. The latter of these proved to be the catalyst for renewed European interest in gliding, which had waned after Lilienthal's death.[4]

During the winter and spring, Bill Tate kept in touch with the Wrights, thanking them for photographs (Miss Baum, especially, was "very much tickled" with hers) and informing them that three-quarters of the population by February was down with influenza as, apparently, were the Wrights themselves. In March he wrote that he was delighted to hear they planned to return to the Outer Banks and trusted they would choose Kitty Hawk again over Nags Head, which they were considering. As requested, he quoted prices for unplaned scantling siding and shingles at Elizabeth City mills. He also made detailed suggestions for the shed they planned to build, proposing that they get a lease from the campground owners including the privilege of selling or removing any structures they erected. He would build the shed himself if they wished.[5]

Bill was pleased to note that there were now two rival vessels "running on the route from here to E City . . . and the service is some better." Israel Perry's boat was not one of them, being "extinct so I was told . . . , the add. you gave him & his Royal Blue passenger service ran him out of business." Tate offered that he would "very much like to help you some provided . . . nothing prevented me." He would be glad to have them stay with him "for a day or two before you get located. . . . Just make yourself at home with me" and "you are welcome to such accomodations & fare as I have." Addie Tate passed along a suggestion that they bring no gasoline stove from Dayton, hers "having not been used since you used it." (So much for Bill's assurance that he had tried it out successfully.) Dan Tate hoped to find regular employment with them at Kill Devil Hills.[6]

The Wrights, having found a reliable person, a skilled mechanic named Charlie Taylor, to run the bicycle shop in their absence, decided to leave early for Kitty Hawk and were en route by July 7, apparently reaching Elizabeth City by evening of the next day. There they were held up briefly by a monstrous hurricane, during which local wind gauges gave way after reaching 107 miles an hour (the strongest ever recorded there). The glider parts, tools, and other supplies arrived from Dayton during the storm on Tuesday, July 9. By Thursday evening the brothers were once again at Kitty Hawk, where they spent the night at Tate's.[7] Neither of them suspected that the hurricane foreshadowed more miseries to come.

The night offered little comfort for the days that lay ahead. The bed provided for them by the Tates sank in the middle so that one occupant had to cling to an edge while the other settled in the trough. Since only the one in the trough could sleep, the brothers changed places several times during the night, the one at the edge having the additional problem of not being able to hold his perch and swat mosquitoes at the same time. The rains had brought a plague of these creatures, "the worst . . . the oldest inhabitant has ever experienced."[8]

The next morning they loaded their gear on a cart and headed for a new campsite at Kill Devil Hills, four miles south. There they set up their tent—the same one used the year before—near the three dunes known as Big Hill, West Hill, and Little Hill (100, 60, and 30 feet high, respectively). These were to be used for the season's glider experiments. An advantage of the location was its proximity to Kill Devil Hills Lifesaving Station. Only three-fourths of a mile distant, its crew of rugged surfmen could, in off-duty hours, provide the brothers with invaluable assistance.[9]

Besides their tent, pitched in a driving rain, they also soon began erecting a tar paper-roofed building as a workshop and hangar. Bill Tate had gone to Elizabeth City and ordered roofing felt, nails, hinges, and such from Sharber and White ("They are reliable people," he promised, "and will treat you fair.") The materials reached Kitty Hawk on July 14 and arrived at camp in a two-horse wagon driven by Tate and George W. Twiford. Framed with two-by-fours by carpenter Oliver O'Neal, the finished structure measured 25 feet long, 16 feet wide, and 6½ feet high. Groceries and other supplies were to be ordered this season from Fulmer and Company, an Elizabeth City grocer and confectioner, so there would be no such ravaging of local shelves as occurred in 1900.[10]

Things went badly from the first day and would continue to do so throughout the season at Kill Devil Hills. Rains made work impossible the next day, and mosquitoes continued to attack with unremitting ferocity. Running out of water and with no well nearby, the Wrights had to collect what rainwater they could from the roof in a dishpan. Their efforts to dig a well during brief breaks in the weather at first proved futile, though eventually they were successful. But "these troubles were nothing," wrote Orville, "in comparison to what was coming." He was sick all Sunday night and kept Will up most of the evening.[11]

Neighbors of the Wrights continued to observe the camp silently from distant windows and were sometimes handsomely rewarded for their vigils. On flightless days the brothers, according to John T. Daniels, would "stand on the beach for hours at a time looking at the gulls flying, soaring, dipping. They seemed to be interested in gannets . . . big birds with a wing span of five or six feet. They would . . . imitate their movements with their arms and hands. They could imitate every movement of the wings of those gannets; we thought they were crazy." Lillie Etheridge recalled that she and others "used to look out the window at them practicing. . . . [t]hey would hold the glider up from the ground on the hill until the wind would catch it up and then it would glide down. They looked just like little children playing, they did."[12]

The Wrights took this photograph of the Kill Devil Hills Lifesaving Station, which stood near their Kill Devil Hills camp, in 1901. The station's crew frequently provided volunteer assistance and hospitality to the Wrights. Three of the crewmen helped launch the first flights on December 17, 1903. *Library of Congress.*

The Assembly of Notables

Chanute's friend Huffaker arrived on July 19 with his small glider. Along with him—and still less welcome—came "a swarm of mosquitoes, which . . . almost darkened the sun." Orville observed: "The sand and grass and trees and hills and everything was fairly covered with them. They chewed us clear through our underwear and socks." Hiding under blankets brought no relief owing to the hot weather: "perspiration would roll off us in torrents." Fires made from old tree stumps created enough smoke to hold back the mosquitoes at times but made the heat still more unbearable. Heavy clothing, mosquito netting, face masks, turbans— nothing appeared to discourage the pests. The plague receded, however, within a few days, during which Dr. Spratt arrived.[13]

The new Wright glider was finished on July 26. The next day it was flown as a kite, with Wilbur on board, in seventeen glides from the slope of the Big Hill. The first eight running starts down the slope with the machine failed to get it airborne. Each time, however, the crew fought off the effects of heat and fatigue to trudge back up the slope for another try. On the ninth effort, the glider successfully bore Wilbur aloft. All the flights in this, as in the previous season, were to be at a level of only a few feet high and lasting only scant seconds each.[14]

Unhappily, the glider proved to be somewhat less manageable than its predecessor. It "refused to act like our machine last year," Orville complained, "and at times seemed to be entirely beyond control." Cross- winds were likely to impair its balance. Spratt, who had done some pertinent laboratory studies, suggested that the builders might have given the wings too much camber. Two more days of tests at the end of July appeared to confirm this judgment.[15]

The wings' front-to-back arch was reduced in a few days at the camp workshop, but there were also other, less obvious problems that must await study in Dayton. Most of Wilbur's thirteen glides made on the next suitable day (August 8) were satisfactory in distance (one reached almost four hundred feet) and other respects. Overall, these were the best results so far. One flight resulted in a stall and Wilbur seemed on the point of crashing, but he managed to bring the machine to a smooth landing by vigorously working the elevator. This seemed to show that the glider could be spared the kind of misadventure that had killed Lilienthal. The new machine also required winds of only about seventeen miles an hour (compared with twenty-five for the old one), so it could be flown more often.[16]

Chanute, meanwhile, arrived on August 4 but, owing to other commitments, remained only a week. Huffaker's efforts to fly the glider he had built for Chanute were so unrewarded that it was soon abandoned and left to rot in the sand. The Tennessean was proving to be a lazy and unpleasant man—more of a liability than an asset—though Spratt was full of good humor and helped pass the time agreeably. Chanute himself was too old to give a hand with the heavy labor, but on most days there was no lack of local assistance.[17]

The crew at the campsite enjoyed the frequent help of Dan Tate and others from Kitty Hawk, including some boys—Jesse and Elijah W. Baum among them—and members of the Kill Devil Hills Lifesaving Station. (Dan Tate's three-year-old son, Sam, sometimes came along and would later recall developing a special fondness for Orville's scrambled eggs.) In particular lifesaver John T. Daniels, a twenty-six-year-old six-footer of considerable strength, was a welcome addition to the work force whenever he could come.[18]

Without becoming meddlesome or intrusive, these sturdy natives provided welcome moments of diversion as well as valuable help. Years afterward, Orville could still smile over surfman Adam D. Etheridge's tying his horse on one occasion to a stake at the campsite, only to have the beast, frightened by the takeoff of the glider, jerk loose and gallop off, leaving Etheridge to walk home. John Thomas (Johnny) Moore, the fortune-teller's son, lived long enough to be reminded many times of his comment concerning the large number of eggs the Wrights had on

(*Left to right*) Octave Chanute, Orville, E. C. Huffaker, and Wilbur at the camp building in the summer of 1901. The glider trials that year proved disappointing, and the Wrights left the Outer Banks on August 20. *Library of Congress.*

hand and Wilbur's startling explanation that their supply was owing entirely to a single hen that laid six eggs a day.[19]

Wilbur was sufficiently encouraged by his latest flights to announce that he would next attempt to make a turn in the air, a thing never successfully done in a glider. In his first flight of August 9 he tried turning, felt his machine growing unstable, and straightened out quickly to avoid a wreck. On his fifth flight of the day, he again tried turning and this time lost control. The glider descended sharply, its left wing striking the ground, then skidded and bounced to a stop. Wilbur suffered facial bruises and seemed lucky not to have broken some ribs. In a final series of flights during three days in mid-August, he had no better luck in turning, though there were no more accidents.[20]

The Wrights recognized that they were faced with at least two serious problems. The first was that the tables of lift (the effect of air pressure on wings set at various angles) that they relied on were wrong. These tables, compiled by researchers over many years, were essential to flying and might require even more years to be put right. The second problem was that their proudest inventions, the elevator and wing-warping apparatus, were, under certain conditions, unsatisfactory and probably even dangerous. Made gloomier by a return of bad weather—four straight days of rain—they decided abruptly that they would close down for the season and take the glider home. They departed on August 20, Dan Tate taking them in a sailboat to Elizabeth City.[21]

Wilbur and Orville had, in fact, reached the point of concluding that there were mysteries to flying that might well be beyond solution. Wilbur, coming down with a cold, barely spoke during the gloomy trip back to Dayton. On one of the few occasions he broke his silence, it was to share with Orville his feeling that the secrets of flight would not be "mastered within our lifetime . . . not within a thousand years." Wilbur was to remark later that, when they left Kitty Hawk in 1901, "we doubted that we would ever resume our experiments. . . . When we looked at the time and money we had expended, and . . . the distance to go, we considered our experiments a failure."[22]

A Better Machine

The discouragement of the 1901 trials, however, vanished almost as soon as the brothers reached home. Within a week Wilbur was locked in lengthy correspondence with Chanute in Chicago on issues of lift, drift, wind resistance, and such. Chanute promptly invited him to address the Western Society of Engineers, one of the country's foremost engineering groups, on September 18. Wilbur accepted and spoke on "Some Aeronautical

Dan Tate and E. C. Huffaker helped launch the second Wright glider. In 1901 Dan became the Wrights' only regular employee on the Outer Banks. He assisted the brothers as general handyman, janitor, and carpenter and in launching glider flights, running errands, and other ways. Wilbur Wright referred to Dan as "the only [work] force we absolutely need." *Wright State University.*

Experiments," summing up much of what he and Orville had learned since 1896. He was now confident, he told his audience, that "when gliders have attained greater skill, they can, with comparative safety, maintain themselves in the air for hours at a time . . . and . . . search out the currents which enable the soaring birds to [fly] . . . by first rising in a circle and then sailing off at a descending angle."[23]

Bill Tate, perhaps sensing the discouragement of the Wrights when they left Kitty Hawk, wrote them in October that "the weather is very pleasant, no mosquitoes. The wind has ruled N. E. average about 20 miles an hour for 2 weeks. I only hope if you ever come to this country [again] you may strike 4 weeks like the past 2 and if you dont fly under those conditions you had better give up the job."[24]

During the winter of 1901-1902 the brothers tackled the problems that had restricted their success of the previous summer. They found almost at once what appeared to be a source of error in standard tables of aerodynamic physics: it was in Lilienthal's calculations of air pressure for measuring lift and drag in wings. Wilbur's figures showed these tables to be based on false information, and he was able to work out from data gathered in his 1901 flights what the proper figures should be. After checking his results with a small homemade wind tunnel, he felt that he was ready to build wings superior to those he or anyone else had used so far.[25]

A second discovery soon afterward, also verified in wind tunnel tests, was that Lilienthal's wings would have been greatly improved by forming their surfaces in the shape of a parabolic curve, one with a gentler camber. Before Christmas the Wrights were eager once more to return to the Outer Banks and test their latest findings.[26]

They went to work on a new and improved glider still larger than the big machine of 1901, its wings spanning thirty-five feet—ten feet more than the previous model. A new feature of the craft was a rear rudder consisting of twin vertical vanes intended to overcome such control problems as Wilbur had experienced toward the end of the 1901 flights. When completed, the new machine bore a radically different appearance from either of the previous gliders, one more like the configuration of the airplanes of later years.[27]

In the summer, Wilbur wrote to George Spratt to invite him to Kitty Hawk for the next trials and to Bill Tate to have him negotiate permission to use once more the Kill Devil Hills campsite rent free. Tate replied with a report that he had obtained permission to use the grounds and erect any new buildings the Wright brothers wished. The summer, he wrote reassuringly, had been dry and mosquitoes the least worrisome in many years. It was arranged that Dan Tate, who had made himself very useful in the summer of 1901, would again be available. In Wilbur's view, his compliance guaranteed "the only force we absolutely need."[28]

Before departing for Kitty Hawk, they also consented to Chanute's request to permit his associate, Augustus M. Herring, to join them. Herring was an experienced glider builder and pilot but—as was soon shown—an egotist with a somewhat jealous streak. Lest he later lay claim to something they invented, the brothers indicated that Chanute ought to be present while Herring was.[29]

A Season of Glad Tidings

Tar Heels living in the Piedmont communities of Winston, Reidsville, and elsewhere had been hearing much of airship experiments in the spring of 1902, but these were unrelated to the glider experiments on the Outer Banks. At Winston, Jacob Hill was drumming up support for a full-sized version of the dirigible a model of which he had on display there; at Reidsville, Louis Kromm was showing off a model of his three-decker airplane and predicting he would soon be flying the government mails.[30] North Carolinians interested in the prospects of aviation were, inevitably,

Daniel M. (Dan) Tate (1865-1905). Half brother of Bill Tate and father of Tom the fisherman, Dan resigned from the Wrights' employment for better income during a big run of fish in the fall of 1903. He was not present at the first successful airplane flight in December. *Courtesy of Daniel Grady Tate.*

more attracted by powered machines than by either the tethered or cordless kites that provided vacation amusement for bicycle mechanics.

The Wright brothers left Dayton on August 25, 1902, once more making their way by train through Norfolk to Elizabeth City. Sister Kate was glad to see them off, having fretted over their "thin and nervous" condition and being convinced—as they were—that life on the Outer Banks did wonders for their health.[31]

At Elizabeth City they purchased lumber for a hangar at Kramer Brothers and Company and took the *Lou Willis* across Albemarle Sound, sleeping on deck overnight. The sixty-foot two-masted schooner belonged to Captain Franklin Harris Midgett of Kitty Hawk. The thirty-eight-year-old Midgett had left the lifesaving service in January to begin forming his own boat line. (Adam D. Etheridge was his replacement.)[32]

It was evident to at least some Kitty Hawkers that the Wrights had shaken off the doubts of the previous summer and now approached their goal with a new determination. Truxton E. Midgett, a hand on the *Lou Willis* and one of the captain's seven children, asked the Wrights whether they expected to fly soon and was told: "Truxton, we don't know if we will fly. But we've studied it, and even if we die trying, we know the principle is sound." The brothers reached Dosher's Wharf at Kitty Hawk on August 29 to begin testing that resolve.[33]

Circumstances conspired to challenge the Wrights' determination before they even started to work. From Kitty Hawk, Dan Tate carried them down to a fishing wharf near the Kill Devil Hills camp in his spritsail boat. From there they set out for their barren campsite on a horse cart furnished by the family of twelve-year-old Jesse J. Baum. In the 1970s Baum recalled the Wrights' arrival and being told by his father to "hitch up Bold'un and I went out to the pasture, caught our big, black horse and hitched him to the cart." En route it became necessary, Baum added, for the Wrights "to get out and push our cart all the way over one hill before we could reach the other one and get to their campsite."[34]

At the camp the tired party found the shed in poor shape. The building, which had been erected in 1901, was drooping at both ends. Harsh winter gales had blown the sand away from the foundations. The brothers spent several days—apparently with lumber bought from Kramer Brothers and delivered via the *Lou Willis*—on repairs and adding space to be used as a kitchen and living room. Beds were installed above the rafters in the attic. Then, sinking a well some ten feet deeper than that of the year before, they located good water.[35]

The brothers' fortunes began improving almost at once. They had brought one of their bicycles to make trips to and from Kitty Hawk easier and faster. The bike, geared for sandy paths and roads, worked even better than they had expected; they could now make the round trip in about an hour, whereas it had previously required three. (Eventually this bike—a sleek black model with chrome trim—was given by the Wrights to Delano F. [Fitzie] Daniels, six-year-old son of John T. Daniels. The bicycle remained in the family for over half a century before rusting into junk.)[36]

By September 8 the Wrights were at work assembling the new flying machine; four days later they made their first tests, getting in some fifty glides over a three-day period. Wilbur began making gentle turns and found that he could do so with no difficulty, bringing cheers from Orville and Dan Tate. "Everything," Wilbur reported jubilantly to Spratt, "is so much more favorable this year than last." They had not seen a dozen mosquitoes in two weeks and their living arrangements were much improved over 1901. They were "having splendid time."[37]

The new glider more than fulfilled the Wrights' expectations. Orville finally began learning to fly, and Wilbur became so proficient that he could bring the machine almost to a standstill in the air without risk of crashing. On September 23, following two rainy days, the brothers made no fewer than seventy-five glides between them. On the last of these, however, Orville made a mistake that caused the craft to nose upward, stall, and begin sliding backward. A moment later there was only "a heap of flying machine, cloth, and sticks," with Orville in the middle of it, amazingly unhurt. "They had guts," Elijah Baum would recall, "they had a lot of crackups. With each wreck they'd get a mouthful or earful of sand, but they never broke any bones."[38]

After a week of repairs, they were back in the air again. By October 2 the brothers were averaging twenty-five flights on good flying days—some for distances of over five hundred feet.[39]

Above and Beyond

Meanwhile, a critical problem appeared in the failure of the new fixed rudder (located at the tail) to prevent such stalling as caused Orville's accident. Kept awake one night by coffee, Orville worked silently through the problem in bed. The next morning he proposed to Wilbur that the rudder be made movable to render the machine more manageable in crosswinds. Wilbur agreed but, reluctant to make the operator responsible for yet another control, proposed that the rudder control and wing warping be performed simultaneously with a single lever. Within a few hours they were at work on the modification, connecting wings and rudder by wires to the warping lever.[40]

Older brother Lorin, his curiosity stirred by so much talk of gliding, showed up unexpectedly on September 30. Spratt arrived the next day on the *Lou Willis;* Chanute and Herring followed on October 5, traveling from Manteo in Tilghman Tillett's sailboat. Until four more bunks were added in the shed's rafters, the guests probably stayed in the homes of Bill Tate and Adam Etheridge. Herring brought with him a glider he had constructed and apprised the Wrights of another on its way—this one built by Charles Lamson, a veteran kite and glider man. Upon their arrival, both machines were found wanting. This was a humiliating discovery for Herring, who considered himself the premier glider builder in America.[41]

The busy comings and goings at Kill Devil Hills at last attracted a flicker of mainland curiosity. On October 3 the Elizabeth City *Weekly Tar Heel* observed that "a colony of inventors" on the Outer Banks, "right at our doors," was engaged in perfecting "[a]erial navigation or the science of flying in mid air by artificial means." The paper continued: "From the wind swept top of a Kill Devil Hill one hundred and twenty feet above the ground, a daring young aeronaut leaps into space and travelling upon a frail machine reaches the ground in safety hundreds of yards from whence he leaped. Next summer he will attach an electric motor and propeller to his contraption and vie with the birds in flight, defying gravity and adverse winds."[42] While evidently not based on direct contact with the aeronauts, the report was reasonably accurate.

After further comments on the gliding experiments, the *Weekly Tar Heel* offered the assessment that the "colony" had "discovered that their machine will work successfully in mid air as long as the wind maintains a velocity of eleven miles an hour. They have perfected a motor and propeller that will drive the machine and all [that] remains is to connect the two. This they are now preparing to do and another year will declare their efforts failure or success. They claim there can be no failure."[43] Having cited the proceedings, however, the paper took no further notice of the Kill Devil Hill experiments.

Activity at the Wright camp quickly became more intense. Dan Tate, now a paid employee, was in and out frequently; he went with Lorin on October 8 to Kitty Hawk to pick up Lamson's glider from the *Lou Willis*. He also ran frequent errands to Kitty Hawk for food, mail, coal oil, nails, and other supplies. Sometimes he brought timely warning from the weather station of approaching storms. Lorin went over to Lillie Etheridge's home one night and got her to make a patch on her sewing machine for a split glider wing. The crew of the lifesaving station sometimes sent over a mess of bluefish or spot. Bill Tate, a surfman at Kitty Hawk since January, had less time for flying than in previous seasons but came by when he could, sometimes staying for meals; he was also involved in a sawmill and lumber operation.[44]

On days when they could not fly, the campers found numerous ways to occupy themselves. The Wrights liked to hunt to supplement their rations. On at least one occasion they bagged a fish hawk to compare the dimensions and proportions of its wings with those of the glider. They also enjoyed target practice, Orville being quite good with a rifle and taking on all challengers. Dr. Spratt spent at least one night at Kitty Hawk with his medical colleague Dr. Cogswell, who now lived at Bill Tate's house and served as postmaster, Tate having moved to nearby Martins Point. (Spratt was glad to return to the camp, having found the bedbugs at Cogswell's almost as unmerciful as camp mosquitoes.)[45]

The Wrights found opportunities for only two or three flights before their visitors left in mid-October. Lorin departed on the fourteenth, Chanute and Herring the next day. Freed of social obligations, the brothers could concentrate more fully on flying and indulge in other activities. On occasions they would go botanizing in the local woods or take walks on nearby beaches in search of starfish, seashells, king crab shells, and other souvenirs for Ohio nieces and nephews. There were signs that the glider men were becoming something of a tourist attraction. One time in late October, an excursion steamer veered off course so its passengers might view some experiments; fortunately, no one came ashore.[46]

Wilbur and Orville made 250 glides in two days after the steamer's visit, setting records for flying in the highest wind they had tried so far (thirty miles an hour), the longest glide by an American (over 622 feet by Wilbur on October 23), longest time in the air (over twenty-one seconds on the same flight), and with the largest machine ever flown. The new rudder worked to perfection. After one of the more impressive flights, Dan Tate offered the opinion that "[a]ll she needs is a coat of feathers to make her light and she will stay in the air indefinitely." Bill Tate, impatient for the main event, is said to have asked, "What in the hell is the matter with you boys; you know that thing will fly, why in hell don't you put an engine on it and *fly*?"[47]

By this time, it was plain to local observers that the methodical Wrights were not given to setting impossible goals for themselves. This became clear, remarked John T. Daniels, "when they got their glider working so they could jump . . . into a wind off that hill and stay in the air for several minutes, gradually gliding down to the beach almost as a gannet could have done it." It began to seem that staring for hours at seabirds and imitating their movements might well have been rational behavior after all. Those who formerly doubted the Wrights' ability to fly a powered machine had now witnessed their dazzling gliding techniques, feats that human beings had never performed before. An Elizabeth City editor had learned that the Wrights were so confident that both now insisted "there can be no failure."[48]

Much of the Wrights' success, Bill Tate was persuaded, resulted from the way they egged one another along in mutual competition. He later recalled that they often "vied with each other in seeing who could best guide the machine down the hill" and "who could best alight . . . on the level land at the foot of the hill." They became so expert that, "after gliding down the hill and getting up considerable speed, they would level out the machine at the foot of the hill, sail out over the level ground, and as the speed slackened, alight on their feet without either wing tip touching the ground."[49]

There seemed to be no special reason why this pleasant kind of activity should not be drawn out for at least several more weeks. Dan Tate, however, gave notice that he would leave on October 27 "to take charge of a fishing crew." Having already performed more than one thousand glides that season, the Wrights agreed that the time had come to go home and build a motored plane. On October 28 they packed away the glider in its hangar and set out on foot for Kitty Hawk.[50]

The return to the mainland was not without complications. Failing to reach Pasquotank River before nightfall, the *Lou Willis* was anchored for the night in the North River. When the wind rose next morning (October 29), Captain Midgett declined to put up his sails; the Wrights had to transfer the next day to the larger *Ray* for a "very rough" afternoon trip to Elizabeth City. But the misadventure could not mask the fact that this visit to the Outer Banks had been by far the most satisfactory of the Wrights' sojourns there.[51]

Word of the growing success of the Kitty Hawk enterprise by now had spread through the aeronautical communities of America and Europe. Scientists and technicians were clamoring for more information on how the Wrights achieved their lengthy flights and remarkable turns; agents of foreign governments had begun making inquiries. There were even overtures from among the latter to buy Wright gliders. It was gratifying to know that their work was appreciated, but the brothers were still well short of their goal and uncomfortable in the limelight. They were determined not to surrender hard-won secrets or set themselves up to be ridiculed in case of ultimate failure.[52]

"Damn'd If They Ain't Flew!"

Upstairs, Downstairs

Almost from the time they began to think seriously about a powered flying machine, the Wrights assumed that installing an engine and propellers would pose no great problems. A steam engine like Professor Langley's might do, but an internal-combustion gasoline engine seemed to have greater possibilities. In the fall of 1902 they wrote to a number of engine builders, including several automobile companies, describing the power plant they needed, but they received no proposals.[1]

In December they assigned to Charlie Taylor, their skilled assistant at the bicycle shop, the task of building a small but powerful gasoline engine. What they needed was a motor that would furnish at least eight horsepower, enough to lift a machine weighing 625 pounds. Taylor's experience was limited to having once helped repair an automobile engine. In six weeks, however, working on the ground floor of the bicycle shop, he completed a 170-pound, four-cylinder engine that was chain driven and air cooled. It tested at a gratifying twelve horsepower; this meant that 150 pounds could be added to the planned flying machine, most of it to strengthen the wings and other parts.[2]

Working on the second floor of the shop, Orville and Wilbur struggled to build the frame for their new machine, relying on three seasons of experience to produce their best aircraft yet. It soon appeared, however, that the propellers, the means of converting the engine's power to thrust, presented major headaches. The Wrights had assumed that they could use what marine engineers knew of boat propellers to design one for an airplane, but they soon found this to be false. There were problems with using propellers in the air that were quite unlike those encountered by marine engineers.[3]

In aircraft the thrust of a propeller depends on the speed of the machine and the propeller itself, the backward flow of air as the machine passes through it, and the angle at which the blades strike the air. The blades must be neither too thick nor too thin. There were also a host of other factors, none of which had ever been carefully studied. Worse still, all these factors were interdependent: an alteration of one meant changes in all the others. Such limited studies as existed were quickly shown to be inaccurate.[4]

As Charlie Taylor could testify downstairs, the complexity of the propeller issue generated heated arguments upstairs. No other problem they had ever tackled approached this one in the demands it made on the Wrights' mathematical skills and technical insights. And it was here that the true measure of their genius asserted itself. Slowly, by using their wind tunnel data and working through a mass of intricate tables and equations, they churned out solutions to the problem. They agreed that they would need two pusher-type propellers, each 8½ feet long and, for the sake of stability, rotating toward one another. The issues of thickness, speed of rotation, blade angles, and other complexities were also gradually resolved. The propellers were to be made of spruce, covered tightly with light canvas, and coated with aluminum paint.[5]

The final designs for the airplane were begun in February 1903. It would be a biplane, somewhat larger than any of the gliders, with a wingspan slightly over forty feet and six feet separating the upper wings

This closeup view of the center section of the 1903 airplane, at the Smithsonian Institution in 1948, shows the propeller drive assembly and controls from the left rear. *National Air and Space Museum.*

from the lower. The pilot, as in the gliders, would lie on the lower wing but slightly left of center to compensate for the weight of the engine, located just to his right. The tail would have a rudder in the form of twin movable, vertical vanes. The whole frame would rest on sledlike twin runners moving along a monorail.[6]

The work was still in progress when Wilbur, again at the invitation of Octave Chanute, addressed the Western Society of Engineers on the 1902 experiments. But he carefully avoided any mention of the powered machine under construction lest newspaper editors, many of whom regarded powered flight as an impossible dream, become inquisitive. The newspapers, he felt sure, would "take great delight in following us in order to record our *troubles.*"[7]

As the brothers made plans to return to the Outer Banks in the late summer of 1903, it became necessary again to fend off Chanute's well-meaning efforts to attach more people to their project. The best they could do, short of outright discourtesy, was to persuade him that they would not have the Kill Devil Hills facilities ready before late October. This settled, they left for Norfolk on September 23. Bill Tate, their loyal steward, had written in July to say he was laid up with an injured thigh from an accident with a gasoline engine, his neighbors incessantly reminding him: "I told you so." As always, however, he was ready "[a]nytime I can be of service."[8]

The injury was more serious than Tate revealed. He had been en route in his new motor launch from Martins Point to Elizabeth City when he stopped at the North River landing to take on a passenger. As he helped the rider aboard, he slipped and fell onto his engine and, according to a report, "had his right leg cut and torn very badly." Dr. Cogswell dressed the wound, yet there remained concern that complications might set in "which could make it serious for him." But Bill kept an appointment to speak at a Kitty Hawk school fund-raiser in early August and did so "in an entertaining and most creditable manner."[9] He was soon fully recovered.

Through Storm and Flame

The Wrights reached Elizabeth City on the afternoon of September 24 and next day caught the steamer *Guide*—a signal improvement in sound crossings—to Roanoke Island. They reached Manteo at midnight and appear to have stayed at the Tranquil House hotel. Next morning they took a gasoline launch to Kitty Hawk and were at the camp by noon. The combination workshop and living quarters was in sad repair, a February storm having torn off boards and pushed away enough sand to cause the ends of the building to settle two feet lower. This meant that a hard rain might flood the floor with up to twenty inches of water. Luckily, the 1902 glider was unharmed.[10]

It was easy to accept Dan Tate's colorful testimony that the storms of the past winter had been the worst in the memory of the oldest Bankers. The winter he described as "one continuous succession of storms of unprecedented severity; the rain . . . in such torrents as to make a lake for miles about our camp." The mosquitoes had been thick enough to turn day into night, the lightning terrible enough to turn night into day. "Nevertheless," Orville concluded, "these sturdy Kitty Hawkers have survived it all, and are still here to welcome us among them."[11]

The hard winter had been followed by a difficult summer on the Outer Banks. On Sunday, July 26, Nags Head's three-story, one-hundred-room Lowe's Hotel was destroyed by fire. Mrs. John Z. Lowe, the proprietor's wife, died of a heart attack during the conflagration. The hotel's chartered steamer, the *Guide*, was reduced from daily to once-a-week service, and the vacation season was temporarily interrupted. Such misfortunes were always damaging to the local economy and could mean suffering for some in the winter that followed. Late summer saw some revival as an engine was installed in the large, shallow-draft sailboat *Hattie Creef* and it began a regular Nags Head run. A godsend to the Wrights, the boat had been built at Manteo by George Washington Creef and was captained by George Creef of the same town.[12]

Despite the adversities of the summertime, the 1903 flying season began well for the Wrights. They struck a bargain with Dan Tate to perform daily work for them at a salary of around four dollars a week, the prevailing local rate for hired help. His chores included washing the morning and noon dishes and helping out—perhaps half a day each week—with the gliding trials.[13] (One senses, though, that the novelty had worn off for Dan and that he was looking for work with better prospects.)

In a hurry to start gliding, the Wrights got the place repaired in two days. The next day, September 26, they began testing the controls of the 1902 machine, which were found to be in good working order. The dunes, though changed in height and position, were in fine shape. On Monday, September 27, they began flying, making seventy-five glides in all and setting a new world's record of slightly over thirty seconds on one of them. Meanwhile, as opportunity allowed, they continued making camp repairs, built an additional shed, and began assembling the new flying machine. (It had not yet been fully assembled, even at Dayton.)[14]

The Wrights experienced a close call when a bad fire in Elizabeth City on September 16 destroyed the Norfolk and Southern freight depot, along with its wharf, some boxcars and track, a steamer, and thousands of dollars in freight. Fortunately, their own orders of tools and groceries were spared by the flames and reached Kitty Hawk on October 7. On September 26 a load of lumber had arrived from Elizabeth City and some fresh eggs were brought in by Dan Tate. Bill Tate and George W. Twiford, a Kitty Hawk farmer, dropped by several times to offer their services.[15]

Apart from their own impatience, the highly publicized experiments of chief rival Samuel P. Langley inspired the brothers to work rapidly. Langley, supported by a hefty army contract, suffered a crash of his powered and manned machine in October but was repairing it for another trial soon. His engine was much more powerful than that of the Wrights, but it seemed to them that his means of control were all wrong, and they doubted that his machine would fly with a man in it. Still, they would have accomplished nothing especially notable at Kill Devil Hills if the Langley venture succeeded first or better.[16]

There was now a steady stream of visitors to the camp. Dan Tate, according to his agreement, appeared regularly and made himself useful as a carpenter and in numerous other ways. Fisherman Walter W. Best and "young Collins" (evidently John Collins's twelve-year-old son Daniel, of Kitty Hawk), on a mission to bring some goods, remained for dinner on the evening of October 8. The Reverend Mr. Davis, Kitty Hawk's Methodist pastor, came down one afternoon with Dan Tate and also took dinner, as did John Moss from Colington Island. Incoming mail, which was delivered to the lifesaving stations, was often brought down to the Wrights on a pony by Kill Devil Hills lifesaver John T. Daniels or Adam D. Etheridge. A Mr. Hollowell invited them to a "theatrical performance" at Kitty Hawk, but the brothers appear to have passed it up.[17]

Parson Davis's interest would seem to indicate that he held few, if any, theological misgivings about the Wrights' assault on the heavens. Half a century before, a barnstorming balloonist had found it necessary to reassure western Carolinians that "persons of the strictest religious principals [sic]" need "fear no repugnance in witnessing any portion of the performance." According to Bill Tate, Outer Banks residents "believed in one good God, a bad Devil, and a hot Hell, and . . . that the same good God did not intend man should ever fly."[18] Nonetheless, no offended Christians showed up to protest the Wrights' effrontery; no strident skeptic appeared to argue the impossibility of flight.

In John T. Daniels's recollection as an old man, the Wrights gradually earned the admiration of the Bankers. At first there had been stealthy snickering over the glider men, even the malediction of a lifesaving station chief that "they ought to be put in a padded cell." At Elizabeth City, Daniels added, similar attitudes were evident when the brothers "were seen on the streets or when material and supplies were seen being loaded in the freight boat" for them. Elizabeth City's newspapers, for the most part, studiously ignored the gliding business from first to last.[19]

Daniels, however, was among those who were impressed that "there was nothing high-hat about the Wrights. They put on no superior airs. They were good company, good mixers with attractive personalities . . . , after we began to know them, one was instinctively drawn to them." Both courteously opened doors and gates for companions, told good stories, and Orville in particular was a fine cook. Daniels boasted of having "had my pedal extremities under their camp table lots of times" and recalled that Orville "could put up as good a meal as any man need want." Elijah Baum admired the Wrights for keeping the Sabbath. "[T]hey never worked on Sunday but didn't mind if a few of us—they didn't like a crowd—visited their camp."[20]

The Blow

On the afternoon of Thursday, October 8, Mother Nature intervened mightily on the side of Professor Langley. A gale struck, according to Wilbur, that "made the storm that followed the prayers of Elijah look small in comparison." The wind began as a mere "breath of air from the south" but soon shifted to the north, reaching about forty miles an hour. There ensued four days of dizzying wind shifts from north to south and east and back again, attended by heavy rains. The wind velocity reached fifty miles an hour on the first night, and the Wrights could "hear the water sloshing around on the floor of our old building." Next morning the winds continued, and the brothers began bracing the new building against them. By 4:00 P.M., however, the storm had reached seventy-five miles per hour and tar paper was ripping loose from the roof of the new building.[21]

Orville, fearing damage to the roof, got a ladder set up at the leeward side of the building and, with Wilbur holding down his flying coattails from below, eventually hammered in enough nails to tame the loose sheets of tar paper. It was slow work, the wind blowing with such violence that the hammer hit his thumb more often than the nails. Next morning the building's floor was underwater. The storm raged on until Monday, October 12. That morning, to no one's real surprise, Dan Tate reported five ships ashore between Kitty Hawk and Cape Hatteras, plus a stranded twenty-foot yawl north of the village. On the twenty-sixth the body of a barge captain, drowned in the storm, washed ashore on the beach opposite Kitty Hawk.[22]

The storm knocked down trees and chimney tops, blew over telegraph and weather station telephone lines, kept boats from leaving Elizabeth City, and interrupted Kitty Hawk's mail service for four days. It also gave Elizabeth City's Democratic newspaper an opportunity to blast President Theodore Roosevelt's administration for the poor wages paid to Outer Banks lifesavers. The brave surfmen, wrote the editor, "faced the storm . . . while the salt spray brought tears to their eyes and the flying sand and pebbles bit like bird shot, still they did not complain."[23]

A new problem arose in late October when Dan Tate showed up at camp with news that the price of fish had gone up, meaning that there was more lucrative work available (with fishing season already well advanced). On October 14 fishermen up the beach at Corolla landed thirty thousand mullet, "the largest catch of fish within memory of men living along the coast." Dan wanted to know how much longer the brothers meant to stay. In the ensuing discussion, he asked for an increase in his wages to seven dollars weekly, his time to be computed from leaving home until his return, and that he receive his money whether there was work for him or not. The Wrights agreed on condition that he remain with them as long as they needed him and that he work ten hours daily, reporting each morning at eight o'clock. The agreement, however, collapsed within a couple of days.[24]

The Wrights, it seems, had come to feel that Dan was not really worth what they paid him. Orville complained in a letter to his sister that Dan was so awkward "that we found it more profitable to let him sit around. Of course he was soon spoiled and even went so far as to complain when any work was wanted on the hill." Things came to a crisis on the cold morning of October 28 when Wilbur asked Dan "to go over to the beach and get some driftwood." Dan refused, proposing that they buy their wood from Jesse Baum at three dollars a cord. When the Wrights persisted, Dan "took his hat and left for home" and was not seen again at camp. Dan's explanation to his family, that the Wrights refused to pay him what they promised, may have been true. He died within two years of his departure from the Wright project.[25]

The lengthy periods of enforced idleness after the October storm were whiled away making repairs on the buildings, adjustments to the flying machines, and visits in the neighborhood. On November 15 Wilbur paid a visit to the Kitty Hawk Lifesaving Station; Orville went to the Kill Devil Hills facility for mail. While at Kitty Hawk, Wilbur also made social calls on Dr. Cogswell and Captain James Hobbs and his English wife, Eliza. (Despite his seventy-four years, Captain Hobbs, a farmer, sometimes did hauling and other work for the Wrights.) Cold weather and Dan Tate's departure forced the Wrights to buy half a cord of firewood and rig a stove out of a carbide can. By general agreement the stove was judged "probably the best . . . in Kitty Hawk."[26]

Alpheus W. Drinkwater, a telegrapher at the Currituck Beach weather station, long afterward recalled one of the Wrights' brief forays from camp. On a late-November morning, Drinkwater took his "one-horse beach cart" over to where some telegraph wires were down. While splicing them,

The subjects in this picture are erroneously identified by the Library of Congress as Bill and Addie Tate. Made by the Wrights, the photograph almost certainly depicts Mr. and Mrs. James W. Hobbs of Kitty Hawk, who were dear friends of the brothers. James Hobbs, a farmer in his seventies, sometimes assisted them in their work. *Library of Congress.*

he recounts, he waved idly at "two figures over on the dunes. They were the Wright brothers."[27]

The pair walked up the beach and stood watching Drinkwater as he worked. "Flown yet?" he inquired. Orville replied that they had not, owing to the October storm and a more recent gale that damaged the camp. "We'll let everybody around here know when we're ready," he added. "I hope you can come." Drinkwater replied that he hoped so, too, but that he was required at this season to be on duty twenty-four hours a day, since his telegrams brought "the tugs down [from Norfolk] to grab ships before they can go on the shoals."[28] Drinkwater's subsequent role in the Wrights' affairs would, as will be seen, become a matter of considerable controversy.

The Moccasin

Kitty Hawk residents sensed that the Wrights must be reaching a moment of destiny in their odyssey at the Kill Devil Hills camp. Like some of the families at Kitty Hawk, surfmen at the Kill Devil Hills Lifesaving Station were near enough to observe what was going on at the camp. "We'd been watching them Wright boys from our window for three years," lifesaver Daniels later recalled, "and visiting them at their camp since they first came down in the summer of 1900 and began experimenting with their funny-looking kites."[29]

Plans to fly the motored machine in early November fizzled out in a succession of frustrating delays. Orville had written home excitedly on October 18 to announce that the new flying machine was nearly finished, and that they had set a world's record by keeping the old one in the air for forty-three seconds. The weather was a factor in ensuing delays, but so was nearly everything else.[30]

Backfiring by the engine damaged the propellers, so their shafts had to be freighted hastily back to Dayton for repairs by Charlie Taylor. Dr. Spratt had arrived at camp on October 23 but, after two weeks of wintry weather, decided to leave; Chanute had come a day later but remained only a week. By mid-November the brothers and their guests had used up all the food they had brought from home. They were reduced to eating crackers and condensed milk before Captain Midgett's *Lou Willis* finally delivered some groceries on November 20, along with the repaired propeller shafts.[31] The shafts had been at Elizabeth City a week with no one to bring them on. Once in place, they worked loose owing to engine vibration. A cement used to fasten bicycle tires to rims corrected the problem. Then came more bad weather: snow as well as rain and, of course, high winds. On November 28 an engine shaft was found to be

Just three weeks before the first successful powered flight, this photograph of the Wright brothers' hangar and their untried flying machine was made at Kitty Hawk— on November 24, 1903. *Library of Congress.*

cracked, and there was no recourse but for Orville to take it home to Dayton for repair.[32]

Abruptly, Kitty Hawk gained the attention of the national press for a story that had nothing to do with flying. On December 3 the submarine *Moccasin*, one of only two such craft in the United States Navy, foundered aground off the beach at Whalehead Lighthouse, thirty miles north of Kitty Hawk. It had parted a navy tugboat's hawser while being towed from Newport, Rhode Island, to Annapolis, Maryland. For telegrapher Drinkwater, it was "the most sensational news story that had ever happened on the Outer Banks" and broke "right in my lap. . . . I looked at her through binoculars and suspected . . . that she must be one of the Navy's wonderful new submarines. . . . The tug was now hovering about the sub as the helpless vessel rolled toward our beach. . . . This was my big break."[33]

Rushing to his telegraph, Drinkwater flashed the news to the Norfolk weather bureau, which relayed it to the navy base at Portsmouth, Virginia. He was waiting on the sand with his telegraph propped on an orange crate that evening when the sixty-three-foot vessel struck the beach. He then wired the navy that the submarine was stranded and "[f]or two weeks I covered myself with glory." The boat was soon mired in six feet of sand, where it resisted the efforts of six tugs to free it, "and every day," Drinkwater continued, "my reputation increased. In order not to miss reporting a single detail about her salvaging I fashioned a tent from an old beach-cart cover and slept on the shore beside her." It was well into January before the boat was worked free. Ironically, it was for this reason that national attention was focused on Kitty Hawk in mid-December 1903.[34]

The Tide Turns

Fortune's pendulum, so long favoring Professor Langley, now swung decisively in favor of the Wrights. When Orville returned to camp from Ohio on December 11, he brought with him the repaired engine shaft and important news: on December 8 Langley's plane, flown by his assistant Charles Manly, had again crashed into the Potomac River. The Norfolk *Virginian-Pilot*, its editorial slant smugly critical of all attempts to fly, chortled in the next morning's headline that the "Buzzard Turned Turtle and Ducked Manly in Icy River." The Wrights congratulated themselves that at least their failures would not be so generally known and mocked.[35]

That local people were anticipating a spectacle of triumph or disaster was evidenced on Sunday, December 13, when Adam D. Etheridge came down from the lifesaving station with his wife and children "to take a look at the machine." (Mrs. Etheridge, née Amanda V. Westcott, was a daughter of Londoner George T. Westcott, who had been shipwrecked years before.) The Wrights had put out word that anyone in the vicinity would be welcome to witness their effort to fly the powered machine. "We knew they were going to fly," John T. Daniels later recalled, "but we didn't know what would happen when they did." The Wrights, determined to be back in Dayton for Christmas, fretted that any further serious delay would end the season without a test of the flying machine.[36]

At 1:30 on the afternoon of December 14, the brothers tacked a large red flag to the side of the new machine's hangar as a signal to the men at the Kill Devil Hills Lifesaving Station. The surfmen understood this meant some flying was to take place and that their help was needed. Those who responded were John T. Daniels (a day laborer before he became a lifesaver in early 1902), fisherman-farmer William S. Dough, Tom Beacham, Robert (Bob) Westcott, and fifty-two-year-old Benjamin W. ("Uncle Benny") O'Neal, all of whom were on hand within a few minutes. With them came several curious boys who had been at the station when the flag went up. The attempt did not create much of a stir at Kitty Hawk, where residents had by now seen many glider flights. Their attention was focused more on the navy's bustling but so far futile efforts to free the *Moccasin*.[37]

The surfmen found that the Wrights had laid a track of two-by-fours sixty feet down the slope of Big Hill and that the seven-hundred-pound flying machine needed to be carried about a quarter of a mile to be placed on it. This was accomplished in half an hour and the plane was placed atop a small "truck," a piece of wood with bicycle hubs attached at the ends as wheels and mounted on the rail. The craft was then tied down on the rail about 150 feet up the nine-degree slope. Wilbur and Orville flipped a coin to determine who would make the first effort, Wilbur winning the honor. It had been agreed, since the fuel tank had enough gasoline for a flight of up to eight miles, that the pilot—if it was feasible—might make a low-level run all the way to Kitty Hawk.[38]

Wilbur eased himself into the belly-bumpums position; the restraining rope was clipped loose, and the plane began to go forward. Orville ran alongside to keep it steady as it moved down the rail but was outrun after about forty feet. (The little boys scampered away, frightened by the deafening sound of the engine.) The machine lifted into the air, nosed sharply upward to about fifteen feet, then slowed, stopped, and dropped back to earth. The harsh landing, no more than sixty feet from the end of the rail, splintered an elevator support. The problem was that the downhill run had caused the airplane to take off too fast. The brief lifting into the wind could not really be called a flight since the distance was so short and the machine had been launched from a slope.[39]

The next day was spent making repairs, the wind falling off too much to attempt any flying. Orville walked over to Kitty Hawk to send home a telegram reporting that a misjudgment at the start had caused the plane to lose power on the first try, but neither brother was discouraged. The message ended: "success assured keep quiet." They were ready to try again on December 16, this time with the track relaid on flat ground within one hundred feet of their old shed. From the level surface, even a brief lift-off into the wind could be considered a legitimate flight. They spent that afternoon awaiting a proper wind, but it refused to come.[40]

During this wait, a beachcomber happened along and asked the Wrights about their unusual machine. Wilbur, who explained that it was intended for flying, was asked if they had flown it yet. The stranger was told that they only needed a favorable wind. After giving the machine a brief inspection, he pronounced his judgment: "I should think that thing *would* fly if you get a suitable wind." Then the stranger wandered off, leaving the Wrights with the distinct impression that he had meant, perhaps, a hurricane. Years afterward, one of the surfmen recalled that the Wrights not infrequently hosted such wanderers "on a long tramp up or down the coast who happened along at meal time."[41]

Forty Yards to Immortality

Thursday, December 17 dawned clear and cold with a chilling twenty-four-mile-an-hour wind from the north. The Wrights remained indoors until around ten o'clock, hoping for a rise in the temperature and a drop in the wind. Finally, with the breeze still blowing hard, they decided to try it anyhow. Once again they set up their signal for the surfmen, who were quickly on hand.[42]

This time the five-man crew included surfman Adam D. Etheridge and his close friend John T. Daniels, thirty-four-year-old William S. Dough, and two others who happened to be at the station, William Cephas (Ceef) Brinkley, a thirty-year-old farmer and lumber buyer, and John Thomas (Johnny) Moore, a lad of seventeen. All except Moore were from Manteo. Brinkley had come over from Roanoke Island the day before to get timbers from a wrecked ship and decided to stay overnight when he learned of the attempt to fly. Young Moore, a trapper and crabber, lived in the Nags Head Woods shack of his widowed mother, Mrs. Mary Moore, the quarter-a-visit fortune-teller for Nags Head vacationers. He had come over for some fishing and "decided to stick around for a while to see the show."[43]

Bill Tate and Alpheus Drinkwater had received personal invitations from the Wrights; but Tate, supposing the wind to be too high for flying, had gone to Elizabeth City on business, and Drinkwater was still manning his makeshift telegraph station up the beach. Lena Tate commented later that it was the great regret of her father's life that he was not present for the flight.[44]

"The Wrights," John T. Daniels recalls, "got their machine out of its shed that morning, and we helped them roll it out to the foot of the big hill, on a monorail. That first plane had only one wheel [at each end] to roll on. . . . It couldn't stand up without somebody supporting it" at both wings. With the machine in place by 10:30 A.M., Wilbur and Orville, in Daniels's words, "walked off from us and stood close together on the beach, talking low to each other for some time. After a while they shook hands, and we couldn't help noticing how they held to each other's hand like they hated to let up, like two folks parting who weren't sure they'd ever see each other again."[45]

Orville and Wilbur walked to the rear of the plane, each spinning a propeller to start the sputtering engine. It was Orville's turn and he climbed onto the lower wing, bracing himself. He shifted his hips about, tested the wing-warping and rudder control, and worked the elevator up and down. Everything was set.[46]

Wilbur, walking over to the spectators, asked Daniels to take over the large box camera that was already set up on a tripod at the right rear of the machine and aimed at the end of the rail. As the plane left the rail, Daniels was instructed, he should press the shutter. Wilbur then placed the camera's black cloth over Daniels's head. "I was told," Daniels recalled, "it is like sighting a rifle. Look in the window . . . and when [the airplane] rises—not *if* it rises . . . just squeeze this thing here."[47]

Turning to the shivering bystanders, who seemed rather grim in the morning's cold ("We were a serious lot," Daniels later commented. "Nobody felt like talking"), Wilbur suggested that they "not look too sad, but to . . . laugh and holler and clap . . . and try to cheer Orville up when he started." With this, Wilbur walked to the right wing and removed a wooden bench that had been set under it to keep the airship from tilting. Orville shifted his gear lever into position to move the plane forward.[48]

It was now 10:35. Orville clipped the restraining wire and moved the machine slowly into the wind, which was measuring up to twenty-seven miles per hour. Wilbur ran along the right side, holding the wing in balance, but, as before, had to release it after about forty feet. As the machine reached the track's end, Orville lifted the elevator and the plane ascended erratically to about ten feet. He was having some difficulty with the elevator, which tended to push the plane first too far one way, then too far the other. This made it rise until Orville altered the control, then dart downward until the next alteration, then lurch upward again. But, humping and swooping along like an indecisive fish hawk, a flying machine was forcing itself forward into the wind for the first time in human history.[49]

A final hump brought Orville down to a skidding halt at a point just over 120 feet from where the machine left the track and after only twelve seconds in the air. But this was all he needed to show that powered flight was not just possible but—at last—a reality. There could be no serious doubt that longer flights could be made in the Wright Flyer and that its power, wings, controls, and other features were sufficient for the tasks required of them. Within moments after he landed, Orville found himself surrounded by the rest, who clamored to offer congratulations. John Daniels, operating a camera for the first time in his life, had just taken what would soon be one of the most celebrated photographs in history. (The Wrights later sent him a copy, which his descendants still treasure.)[50]

Daniels's memories of the historic moment, colored and clouded by the hindsight of twenty-nine years, were that the onlookers "helped steady [the plane] down the monorail until it got under way. The thing went off with a rush and left the rail as pretty as you please, going straight out into the air maybe 120 feet when one of the wings tilted and caught in the sand, and the thing stopped."[51]

From the distance of almost a century, it is impossible to gauge precisely the reactions of witnesses to the culminating event. Daniels in 1932 offered an interviewer a description that bordered on the poetic: "I don't think I ever saw a prettier sight in my life. Its wings were braced with new and shining copper piano wires. The sun was shining bright that morning and the wires just blazed in the sunlight like gold. The machine looked like some big, graceful golden bird sailing off into the wind. I think it made us feel kind o' meek and prayerful like."[52]

But Daniels, alas, could tailor his emotion nimbly to his audience. In 1943 he wrote with more credibility that "[t]he flight didn't last long. I didn't think it amounted to much," or, as he put it on another occasion, "yes, we cheered him all right, but there were only about six of us and we didn't make much noise and, besides, we were used to seeing the glider go up, so we weren't much impressed."[53]

One must admire the candor of that view of the matter. What the witnesses had seen was nothing in comparison with the lyrical agility of a gull intent upon catching a bread crumb tossed from a boat. A rare vision was required to transmute those twelve seconds into a grand historic moment.

A sense of awe, an immediate recognition that men had performed what many thought could never be done, is distinctly lacking in the witnesses' reflections of later years. Elijah Baum, Wilbur's first human contact on the Outer Banks, told interviewers as an old man that he missed the flight because he "didn't think it was worth the walk from Kitty

The first flight, December 17, 1903, with Orville at the controls and Wilbur standing to the right. Lifesaver John T. Daniels took this photograph as the plane left its launching track at about 10:35 A.M. It was the first time he had ever snapped a picture, but the image is one of the most famous in the history of photography. *Library of Congress.*

Hawk." (It was not apparent that he had changed his mind since!) Johnny Moore, an honored guest at the Smithsonian's unveiling of the Wright Flyer in 1948, scarcely glanced at it, commenting dryly to reporters: "I seen it once." On behalf of Kitty Hawk housewives who might have glimpsed the flight, Mrs. Jesse E. Baum assured journalists in her advanced years that onlookers were chiefly concerned about the buzzing airplane's effect on the livestock and chickens.[54]

These were not the responses of people who assumed that the Wrights were crazy to think they could fly. Bankers who, then or later, spoke so of the first flyers appear to have had in mind their antics in rushing back and forth across the sand simulating bird movements or staring for hours at seabirds. John T. Daniels once remarked that people "laughed at them as just a pair of poor nuts. . . . They would sit on the beach for hours, just watching the gulls." To the natives, *that*, rather than trying to fly, was behavior unworthy of adults. As Daniels's daughter Mellie put it, "[a] lot of folks thought the Wrights were a little touched, you know. I think it was because they would imitate the way birds flew . . . turn their arms like wings and run through the dunes while watching the gulls."[55]

Apart from Wilbur and his five assistants, others subsequently claimed to have witnessed the first flight and were situated to have done so. One, surfman Bob Westcott of the Kill Devil Hills Lifesaving Station, was watching the proceedings from time to time through a spyglass. Another, Captain S. Joseph Payne at the Kitty Hawk station, four miles distant, also had his binoculars trained on the scene. The honor was subsequently claimed in addition by Kitty Hawkers George A. Tillett and Clarence Twiford, both later residents of Elizabeth City, who were small boys in 1903.[56]

It seems likely that there may have been still other witnesses. Dan Simpson, a cook at the Kitty Hawk Lifesaving Station, was said to have seen part of the flight from his kitchen window. Astonished by the sight, he "dropped the batter for two pancakes into his hat (which was on a chair) instead of onto the stove."[57] It was a nice tale, but four miles was much too far for Dan's naked eye.

The First Airplane Casualty

The first flight was too short to silence all critics and rivals of the Wrights; the brothers knew they could not return satisfied to Dayton without attempting a more impressive demonstration. There were a few minutes of good cheer around the Wrights' stove before the Kill Devil Hills company set out for another trial of the airplane. At 11:20 A.M. Wilbur took the controls and flew 195 feet. Orville tried again and was able to cover about 200 feet in fifteen seconds in the air. At midday Wilbur made a wonderful flight of 852 feet, remaining airborne for fifty-nine seconds, a feat few skeptics could dismiss. Wilbur's flight was the last of the day. His takeoff was good, but he "got too close to a sand knoll," Daniels recalled, "and the rudder came off. I was standing on the lee side of her. . . . I jumped and tried to pull her down . . . I was lifted off the ground . . . and fell back into a sand dune."[58] Daniels, soon to become the first airplane casualty, might have laid claim at that point to having been the first airplane passenger as well!

Swept up by the success, the group began discussing a flight to the Kitty Hawk weather station, from whence a telegram might be sent to Dayton over Dosher's wires. Suddenly, however, their optimistic plans changed. According to John T. Daniels,

They were going to fix the rudder and try another flight when I got my first—and God help me—my last flight. A [35-mile-per-hour] breeze . . . swept across the beach just like you've seen an umbrella turned inside out and loose in the wind. I had hold of an upright of one of the wings when the wind caught it and I got tangled up in the wires that held the thing together. . . . I found myself caught in them wires and the machine blowing across the beach, heading for the ocean, landing first on one end and then on the other, rolling over and over and me getting more tangled up in it all the time. I tell you I was plumb scared. When the thing did stop for half a second, I nearly broke up every wire and upright getting out of it.[59]

The startled onlookers, fearing the worst, rushed to Daniels's aid. "I wasn't hurt much," Daniels continued. "I got a good many bruises and scratches and was so scared I couldn't walk straight for a few minutes. But the Wright boys ran up and pulled my legs and arms, felt of my ribs and told me there were no bones broken. They were scared, too. The machine was a total wreck. The Wrights took it to pieces . . . and gave us a few pieces as souvenirs." Wilbur wrote in his diary that evening that Daniels's "escape was miraculous as he was in with the engine and chains." (Orville in later years introduced Daniels at a banquet as "[t]he man . . . who rode further in the plane than either of the inventors.")[60]

Onlookers were surprised and relieved to find that Daniels was not seriously hurt, but it was also clear that the flying was finished for 1903. The Wrights and their crew dragged the wreckage back to the hangar and decided to crate it for shipment to Dayton. After lunch, the brothers walked up to Kitty Hawk to send home a telegram that had long been awaited.[61]

In the meantime the proud surfmen, chatting animatedly about what they had seen, made their way back to the lifesaving station. For many years afterward they would relish retelling how young Johnny Moore, spotting Bill Tate (or somebody else) hurrying along the beach toward the camp, called out loudly to him: "They done it! Damn'd if they ain't flew!"[62]

Yellow Journals, Purple Prose

Newspapers for the most part had ignored the Kill Devil Hills experiments, though occasionally there were dispatches mentioning the Wrights' box kites and gliders. The Raleigh *News and Observer*, for example, picking up the Elizabeth City *Tar Heel*'s article, reported in October 1902 that the brothers were soaring nearly 120 feet high for hundreds of yards and planned to attach an electric motor to their flying machine in 1903. The glider, however, was described as "a flimsy box-kite affair with a number of silken wings and steering attachment of like material."[63] The heavens seemed safe enough from such an intruder.

The first newspaper to send a reporter to Kitty Hawk was apparently the *Asheville Citizen*, whose editor hoped to get an amusing tale for his readers. In early December 1903 the *Citizen* editor directed Ora L. Jones, a young reporter who had shown some comic talent in writing a spoof of the Langley experiments, to go to the Outer Banks, where "two cranks were trying to fly." With fifty dollars of the paper's money in hand, Jones made his way to Kitty Hawk, five hundred miles east, with a mandate to "write some really funny stuff."[64]

Arriving there, Jones, by his account, introduced himself to the Wrights and was told by them that they "wanted no publicity. They ordered me to get away from Kill Devil Hill and stay away." Retreating in dismay, Jones borrowed a telescope at the Kill Devil Hills Lifesaving Station and was able to observe some of the Wrights' work at a distance. But cold weather, cutting sand, insects, and bad food quickly led him to doubt that "the Wrights could ever fly, so I decided to go home." The day was December 17.[65]

Jones was passing through Goldsboro a day or so later—probably December 19—on his way to Asheville when he saw a piece in a Raleigh paper about the first successful flight. "Ironically," he later wrote, "that flight took place while I was sitting by a tin stove in my boarding house a mile from Kill Devil Hill, impatiently waiting for the horse and buggy to take me back to Elizabeth City." Apparently he wrote no account of his trip for the *Citizen*.[66]

Harry P. Moore, head of the Norfolk *Virginian-Pilot*'s mail room in 1903, claimed in later years that he first learned of the glider experiments in the fall of 1900. His informant was said to have been a beachcomber sent to Norfolk by the Wrights to buy a barrel of Lynnhaven oysters. After that Moore allegedly visited Kitty Hawk, met the Wrights without disclosing to them his newspaper connection, and was allowed to observe some of their glider trials. By his account, Moore arranged for John T. Daniels, Adam Etheridge, and Joe Dosher to keep him informed of developments: "Every time they pulled their gliders up Kill Devil Hill," Moore insisted, "I soon knew it."[67]

Moore maintained that he received a telegram from Dosher on the morning of December 17, only minutes after the second powered flight. It read: "Wrights flew in motor-driven machine 11:20." Later in the day Moore allegedly spoke by the weather bureau telephone with Daniels and Etheridge, who verified that "[o]ne of those fellows flew just like a bird. The two of them put gasoline in the engine in their contraption, and after it glided down the hill in a wooden truck it went up. It was Orville that flew, and he came down safely."[68] (There had been no downhill run, of course, one of several discrepancies that tend to undermine Moore's veracity.)

Meanwhile Wilbur and Orville, anxious that the first public announcement of their success should come from Dayton, were unaware of any earlier report. They arrived at the Kitty Hawk weather station around 3:00 P.M., where Orville wrote out this brief telegram to their father, Bishop Wright: "Success four flights thursday morning all against twenty one mile [*sic*] wind started from Level with engine power alone average speed through air thirty one miles longest 57 [*sic*] seconds inform Press home Christmas." Joe Dosher, silent in regard to the alleged late-morning telegram, tapped out the message, requesting the Norfolk station to telephone it to Western Union. Dosher made "almost immediate contact" with Norfolk.[69]

Before the Wrights could leave the station, a reply came from Charles Grant, a messenger at the Norfolk weather bureau, asking whether the news might be shared with a reporter from the *Virginian-Pilot*. The Wrights responded that it was to be shared with no one. They then stopped by the lifesaving station, where Captain S. Joseph Payne boasted to them of seeing the flight through his binoculars. They also stopped at the post office, where they chatted briefly with old Mr. Hobbs and paid a farewell visit to Dr. and Mrs. Cogswell before returning to camp.[70]

At about five o'clock in the afternoon Edward O. Dean, a *Virginian-Pilot* reporter, made a routine call to the Norfolk weather station to inquire about any news of interest and was informed by Grant—despite his instructions to the contrary—of the Kill Devil Hills flights. Dean was discussing with his editor whether to seek confirmation and further details when the young man from the mail room, Harry P. Moore, came in with a more substantial account of the Wrights' success. There appeared to be no question that something of considerable importance had occurred at Kitty Hawk.[71]

City editor Keville Glennan was in something of a dilemma. Seven months earlier Charles P. Sapp, the *Virginian-Pilot*'s editor, had written an editorial condemning the dangerous experiments of aeronauts such as Langley and pointing out the unlikelihood that machines could be made to fly. Even if they could, Sapp had concluded, they would never be able to compete with ships and railroads for speed and safety. When the *Charlotte Observer* promptly replied with a defense of aeronautical experiments and its firm belief that man would yet fly, Sapp responded in cool contempt, accusing the *Observer* of believing not only in flying machines but in "the conserving qualities of the left hind leg of a graveyard rabbit killed in the dark of the moon." Even within the past few days, of course, the *Pilot* had made considerable sport with Langley's latest fiasco.[72]

Liberally embellishing the reports of Moore and Dean, Glennan put together for the next morning's newspaper a tale that was thus replete with errors and exaggerations, but it was a coup that made journalistic

After their successful flight on December 17, the Wrights visited Kitty Hawk Lifesaving Station, where Capt. S. Joseph Payne reported that he had watched the event, four miles away, through his binoculars. By the time this photograph was taken, the station had been altered in appearance and superseded by the building in the background. *Courtesy of the Outer Banks History Center, North Carolina Division of Archives and History, Manteo.*

history. The front page for December 18 announced in a banner headline "FLYING MACHINE SOARS 3 MILES IN TEETH OF HIGH WIND OVER SAND HILLS AND WAVES ON CAROLINA COAST."[73] Ironically, then, the *Virginian-Pilot*, skeptic that it had long been of aeronautical science, became the medium for breaking to the world the news of the dawn of aviation.

In a follow-up report on December 19, the *Virginian-Pilot* underscored its new attitude toward flight by praising the dirigible-building Hill brothers of Stokes County, who had earlier been scorned in its columns. "North Carolina," the paper now acknowledged, already laid "claim to an inventor who has conquered the air in the person of two brothers named Hill, of Wilkes [*sic*] County who have erected a contrivance that they plan to take to St. Louis next year and compete for the grand prize. . . ."[74] The *Virginian-Pilot*, having found mechanical birds unpalatable in May, thus found itself eating crow in December.

Meanwhile, on the evening of December 17 Lorin Wright carried his brothers' wire to Dayton's Associated Press office for transmission to newspapers around the country. Associated Press representative Frank Tunison replied dismissively to Lorin that fifty-seven seconds in the air was not a news story, though fifty-seven minutes might be. (AP finally did send out an abbreviated version of the story the next day.)[75]

The *Virginian-Pilot*, on the evening of the first flights, sent offers to twenty-one major newspapers to sell a condensed version of the story, but only five bought it. Of these, just one, the *Cincinnati Enquirer*, gave it front-page prominence. A call from Norfolk to a Dayton morning paper, the *Journal*, elicited an answer that the editor did not "want any cock and bull yarn like that." Dayton readers learned the story from afternoon papers on December 18, the *Daily News* carrying it in a neighborhood news section under the misleading head "DAYTON BOYS EMULATE GREAT SANTOS-DUMONT."[76]

Alpheus Drinkwater, the telegrapher covering the rescue of the submarine *Moccasin*, later claimed to have had a role in sending the Wrights' telegram. He declared that the telegraph wires were down at the time and Dosher had to relay messages through Drinkwater's outpost on the beach near the settlement of Corolla. "Charley Grant," Drinkwater wrote in 1948, "kept asking questions about the flight, [for a] description of the machine that had made it and so on, right up to midnight. I would relay his messages to Joe Dosher and he would give me the information. . . . His knowledge was mostly hearsay. . . . [He] had not even bothered to go over to Kill Devil Hill to see them make the experiment."[77]

Drinkwater's claim to have relayed the Wrights' telegram appears to be false (perhaps unintentionally so), though it is possible that he was one of those Outer Bankers besieged by the newspapers for information. His remoteness from Kill Devil Hill at the time may account for many of the

distortions in the *Virginian-Pilot*'s account. Harry Moore's claims have
also been refuted by veteran *Pilot* editor Robert Mason, whose research
indicates that Moore's information reached him from the same source as
Edward O. Dean's—the Norfolk weather station—and on the same
evening.[78]

The *News and Observer* and several other North Carolina newspapers,
including the *Charlotte Observer*, carried the brief Associated Press account in their December 19 editions, but most of the state's papers
ignored the story altogether. The *Wilmington Star* hinted broadly that
the report might well be just another hoax. On Christmas Day, editor
D. A. Tompkins of the *Charlotte Observer* stated with satisfaction that his
paper had been receiving congratulations owing to its longtime faith in
the coming of powered flight. He was also pleased that the event had taken
place on the coast of North Carolina, "the home of the newspaper which
has consistently maintained, amidst universal despair, that we would yet
fly."[79]

At Kill Devil Hill on the morning of December 18, the Wrights began
disassembling the airplane and crating it for their return to Dayton.
Around noon the next day, Captain Jesse E. Ward, a Kitty Hawk surfman,
appeared at the camp with a telegram: the Norfolk correspondent of the
New York *World* was seeking exclusive rights for a story with pictures. Not
long afterward, John Daniels came over with several more telegrams,
including requests from the *Woman's Home Companion*, *Scientific American*, and *Century Magazine*. But the Wrights decided to decline all such
proposals. In Dayton, more reporters were descending on the Wright
home.[80]

The brothers, with their airplane, appear to have left Kitty Hawk on
the morning of December 22 aboard the schooner *Nancy Hall* and
reached Norfolk by rail from Elizabeth City via Suffolk. Reporters rushed
to Norfolk from distant places to interview them and learned that they
were lunching at Lynn's Restaurant. While two gentlemen named Mason,
sitting at the front of the restaurant, were identified by a waiter as the
Wrights and duly besieged, the inventors dined quietly in the rear and
escaped detection. They were said to have avoided journalists elsewhere
in Norfolk by using decoys. After buying a barrel of Lynnhaven oysters,
they left for Dayton, where they arrived on the evening of the twenty-
third.[81]

The elusiveness of the Wrights was perhaps the reason Bill Tate
returned from his Elizabeth City trip to find telegrams from the *New York
Journal* offering him "good pay" for a six-hundred-word article on the
first flights and from the *Norfolk Dispatch* for five hundred words.
Although "sorely tempted," as he wrote Wilbur, Tate declined the offers.
He was sorry, he wrote, that "Dan played the fool & left you. He evidently

does not know what is best for him." (It appears, then, that Bill had not seen the Wrights since late October.)[82]

If the brothers worried much about the ill effects of instant celebrity, they might have spared themselves the trouble. Aeronautical circles were not easily persuaded that newspaper reports could be trusted, and the public at large quickly shifted its interest to other matters. It was to be years yet, prolonged by the Wrights' own penchant for secrecy, before it was generally acknowledged that powered flight had become a reality.

CHAPTER SIX

Keeper of the Flame

A Lean Harvest

The Wright family of Dayton, Ohio, enjoyed a notably happy Christmas in 1903 as accolades poured in from near and far for the achievement of Wilbur and Orville. On December 26 Bill Tate wrote to mention that he had been at Elizabeth City on the day they flew and to inform them that Norfolk and Elizabeth City newspapers had since carried articles about the flight. He was sorry not to have been more at "Camp Wright" but "was very busy all the time." He hoped their stay there had been pleasant and, as ever, wished to know "[i]f I can be of service to you any time." He was to remain in close touch until Orville's death in 1948.[1]

The brothers were already discussing their next steps. Critics who carped that a flight of less than a minute was something short of a revolution in travel had a point. The Wrights had so far spent a total of only ninety-eight seconds in motorized flight. The Wright Flyer might suggest a delightful hobby for wealthy sportsmen but could be nothing more until it was improved to the point of practical utility—and financial compensation for its builders. Kitty Hawkers themselves may have felt twinges of disappointment if they saw an Associated Press dispatch in early 1904 in which the Wrights stated that all of their experiments had been "conducted at our own expense, without assistance from any individual or institution."[2] They presumably meant financial assistance, but the statement still appeared to lack generosity.

Anticipating other aircraft builders' incorporating their ideas, the brothers began the tedious process of applying for a patent broad enough to encompass almost every imaginable sort of flying machine. Chanute and others urged them to enter their plane in the St. Louis Exposition, but the Wrights wanted no public demonstrations before their patent was granted—and that would not come until 1906.[3]

In order to continue experiments without the expense of repeated trips to North Carolina, the Wrights established a new test site in early 1904, eight miles east of Dayton. There, at a secluded one-hundred-acre rural pasture known as Huffman Prairie, they developed their new air-plane. Despite a more powerful engine, the new machine proved to be less satisfactory than that of 1903. Its flights were limited to short hops, partly owing to Ohio's uncertain winds. (Kill Devil Hills had spoiled them in that regard.) This problem was solved with a system of catapult launching. By the end of the summer, the Wrights had achieved a flight of nearly a mile, lasting over a minute and a half. Accidents were frequent, however, and control of the plane was chancy at best.[4]

A third plane, begun in the spring of 1905, also turned out to be disappointing. After its elevator was enlarged and moved further forward, matters began to improve dramatically. In August Orville was able to remain aloft for almost five minutes at a time; in September for over eighteen minutes; in October for nearly forty minutes. (The belly-bumpums position of the pilot having become intolerable on such flights, the Wrights would hereafter fly in a sitting position.) It required no great effort to think of military applications for a plane that could remain this long aloft. By now there were signs of keen interest on the part of several governments, including those of the United States, Britain, and France.[5]

Eager to begin capitalizing on their invention, the Wrights set out in the fall of 1905 to find parties or governments willing to buy airplanes from them. In doing so, however, they guarded against possible theft of their ideas. They rejected potential buyers who demanded first to witness a performance of the Wrights' plane, examine it, or be provided with its specifications before making offers. The inventors even declined to pro-vide photographs of their machine. For this reason, negotiations with government agencies were difficult and, for a long time, fruitless.[6]

Rumors began to circulate suggesting that the Wrights might have concocted their stories of flying in North Carolina and Ohio. In January 1906 the prestigious *Scientific American* magazine published an editorial casting doubt on their flights. The *New York Herald* followed with a February article that raised the issues of whether "[t]he Wrights have flown or they have not flown. They possess a machine or they do not possess one. They are in fact either fliers or liars." This sort of criticism tended further to complicate negotiations with prospective customers. Mean-while, news came from France, Denmark, and elsewhere of successful short powered flights by various inventors. The gap between the Wrights and their rivals was rapidly closing.[7]

One of those rivals was Dr. William W. W. Christmas of Washington, D.C., a native of Warrenton, North Carolina. Dr. Christmas, whose claims remain in dispute, is said to have begun to experiment with gliders in 1905. In early March 1908 he supposedly flew his motored biplane, the *Red Bird*, for a distance of about one hundred feet across a field on the Robert Nevins Ions farm near Fairfax Station, Virginia. The claim has never been adequately substantiated, but, if true, it would make Christmas the first American after the Wrights to make a powered airplane flight. He was, definitely flying his own planes by 1909 or 1910.[8]

At Kitty Hawk, Bill Tate devoured all he could find in periodicals on the Wrights and their competitors and continued to hope they might find reason to return to his neighborhood. A letter from him in the summer of 1906 asked pointedly if they planned to return; if not, he would like to have their main building for a neighbor and would be happy to send them anything they might have left inside it. His wife and daughters sent "kindest wishes & often think of you & call back the stay you made in our community & the fun we had as very pleasant recollections."[9]

Another applicant for use of the camp buildings was Adam Etheridge, who wrote that they were "sanded up pretty bad and open and soon will come to nothing you cant keep them shut they are wrecked up bad." Etheridge wished "to build a [fishing] camp" of his own for the spring season. He, and no doubt Tate as well, was informed by the Wrights that they expected to use the building again and did not wish to dispose of it. The brothers began sending Etheridge a five-dollar annual retainer to watch over the camp and to keep them informed in regard to its condition.[10]

A Spring on the Outer Banks

By early 1908 Bill Tate informed the brothers that transportation between Kitty Hawk and the mainland had undergone much improvement since the days of Israel Perry. Having finally conquered his fear of gasoline engines, Bill was now the proud owner of "the best & fastest launch in N. C." and could, if they ever came back, pick them up himself at Elizabeth City. Captain Midgett was running his own powerboat three times weekly between Elizabeth City and Kitty Hawk.[11]

If they did return, Tate promised, they would find other notable changes. Tom Tate had grown into "a very steady boy" and an entertaining raconteur of tales about his hunting prowess. Irene and Lena were in school and able to attend eight months of the year. Dan Tate, fisherman and hunter, had died in October 1905; the old Hobbses were feeble; Dr. Cogswell had moved to Manteo. Soon Addie's father, Elijah Sibbern, was also gone. The Wright camps had blown down and the lumber and contents were mostly gone. Bill thought he could recommend, anyhow, a better site some eight miles up the coast.[12]

The French government, worried over the prospect of war with Germany, began to show interest in buying Wright airplanes. Although Wilbur spent several months in France in late 1907, he returned home in

December without getting a contract. By the spring of 1908, a return to Kitty Hawk, the fountainhead of their success, seemed just the right tonic for the Wrights' doldrums. To prepare for important forthcoming tests before prospective American and foreign buyers, the Wrights felt they needed more privacy than was possible at Huffman Prairie. The primary goal of the trip would be to ascertain whether their newest machine could meet performance requirements for a plane being sought by the United States Army.[13]

Wilbur came first, arriving at the old camp in early April to prepare it for Orville's arrival with their newest flying machine later in the month. He spent the night at Elizabeth City's Southern Hotel on April 7; the next day he bought some lumber at Kramer Brothers mill, hardware at White's store, and gasoline at Grandy's. He also ran into John T. Daniels, lately transferred to the Nags Head Lifesaving Station. After a two-day wait, he took Captain Franklin Midgett's gasoline launch, the *B. M. Van Dusen*, for Kitty Hawk and sent some lumber on the sailboat *Lou Willis*, now commanded by Captain Midgett's son Spencer. The rest of his lumber was not yet ready and was to be sent on in a few days.[14]

At Kill Devil Hills, Wilbur at first found only rubble and vexation. After a night at Captain Midgett's, he reached the 1903 camp on the morning of April 11 in Spencer Midgett's pony cart, finding only some roofless walls of his old hangar, a foot of sand and debris covering the floor, and scattered remains of the 1901, 1902, and 1903 flying machines. The building put up in 1903 was "torn to pieces," victim of a Christmas storm, and it appeared that some boys on vacation had torn out the cots and taken away whatever seemed both interesting and portable. Captain J. E. Ward, now at the Kill Devil Hills Lifesaving Station, offered Wilbur a place to sleep until he could get a new building up.[15]

The Kill Devil Hills lifesavers now included, besides old hands Westcott, Dough, and O'Neal, new recruits W. O. Twifert, Walter W. Midgett, and Willis Tillett. Westcott was perhaps the most intriguing of the crew, regaling Wilbur with his plan for a "perpetual motion machine," a kind of steam engine that would, as Wilbur understood it, "practically eliminate the necessity of fuel or at least reduce the quantity to insignificant proportions."[16] Few such notions could be summarily dismissed now that powered flight was a reality.

Troubles continued. On April 12 Augustus Harris and Spencer Midgett began carting some lumber from the old fish wharf near Kill Devil Hills, to which Truxton Midgett and his uncle Ezekial Midgett had lightered it from Kitty Hawk. Oliver O'Neal and Jesse Baum were hired as carpenters, but the work went slowly owing to a succession of mishaps. Boat service was interrupted when the *Lou Willis* lost her sails in an April 11 storm near the mouth of the Pasquotank and then grounded when the water was blown out of Hayman's Bay (near Kill Devil Hills). Two more days were lost to bad weather, during which Wilbur came down with intestinal flu and had to stop work. Meanwhile, the Kramer mill was tardy in its deliveries of lumber.[17]

Fortunately Charlie Furnas, a Dayton mechanic interested in flying, showed up unexpectedly on April 15 to lend a hand. (He also found lodging with the lifesavers.) On Saturday, April 18, Wilbur, still suffering from the flu, walked ten miles round trip to Kitty Hawk. There he offered to pay Captain Midgett to make a special trip in his launch to Elizabeth City for lumber. Wilbur followed this up with a telegram to the mill to have the lumber ready at the wharf when Midgett arrived.[18]

The twenty-dollar payment for what ordinarily would have been a six-dollar load of lumber was a memorable transaction in the lives of the Midgett family. Truxton Midgett tells it this way:

We were to have a special service at our church the next day [Easter Day] and as Uncle Will was Superintendent of our Sunday School, also cook on the Van Dusen, we nevertheless left him behind so as to be sure he would be on hand the next day, Easter. So I agreed to cook, and we got under way as soon as possible. We had a good run that day and arrived in Elizabeth City in time to load the lumber that afternoon. We left town the next morning (Sunday) at 3 o'clock and made it home in time of Easter Service. We delivered the lumber Monday a. m. as agreed and we all felt good.[19]

Wilbur, however, was irked almost beyond endurance. On Saturday evening he wrote in his diary, "[c]onditions are now almost intolerable." His lumber reached the fishing wharf on Monday, but it failed to rescue Wilbur from his gloom.[20]

Matters improved when Orville arrived with the latest airplane, a version of the 1905 model, on April 25, just in time to move into the new building. The machine's arrival sped work at the camp. Ward and Westcott came over from the station the next day to lend a hand, as did George Baum from Kitty Hawk. Bill Tate and Walter Best paid a visit on May 3; Benny O'Neal, Captain Ward, and Willis Tillett were in and out. The plane was assembled by the end of April. By now the newspapers had learned of the new tests. Reporters from the *New York Herald*, *New York American*, London *Daily Mail*, and other periodicals converged on the Outer Banks and established Manteo's Tranquil House hotel as their base.[21]

Flights began on May 6 with Orville at the controls. The next day Wilbur flew over twenty-two hundred feet, staying up for about a minute. There were more flights on subsequent days, one for over two minutes. On May 14 Charlie Furnas, flying with Wilbur, became the world's first airplane passenger. This was one of several flights that lasted for over four minutes and covered almost a mile. On the day's last flight, with Wilbur at the controls and Furnas his passenger, the plane crashed near Little Hill.

It hit the sand at forty-one miles an hour, leaving both men with ugly abrasions but no bones broken. Although none of the flights covered as much as 2½ miles, many newspapers, the *Virginian-Pilot* among them, generously credited the Wrights with aerial voyages of 18, 24, and 32 miles.[22]

The crash brought a sudden end to the 1908 trials, but the Wrights had learned what they came to find—that their machine was capable of meeting the army's specifications. Wilbur dashed off for Manteo, where he caught the *Hattie Creef* for Elizabeth City and then headed for France. Orville, remaining briefly to close down the camp, was soon off to Washington for further negotiations with army officials.

In France during the winter and summer, Wilbur dazzled witnesses with his powered flights, demonstrating that his machine was far superior to those of France itself. Meanwhile, at Fort Myer in Virginia Orville was showing the army what could be done with an airplane. The inventors' pall of silence was finally lifted and the world was brought face-to-face with the technical prowess of the Wrights.[23]

Payoffs from the latest Kill Devil Hill trials came quickly. The army had advertised for a plane that could carry two men 125 miles at forty miles per hour, remain aloft for an hour, and land undamaged. On September 11 at Fort Myer, Orville made a flight of over an hour with a passenger, but on September 17 he suffered a crash. He was injured and knocked unconscious, his passenger dying of a fractured skull. The army's interest, however, did not wane.[24]

Wilbur, in the meantime, was winning aerial prizes and honors in France. On October 7 he took Mrs. Hart Berg for the first airplane flight by a woman. In Rome not long afterward, a newsreel cameraman with Wilbur took the first motion pictures made from an airplane in flight. In March, French investors agreed to terms to buy the Wrights' French patents and licenses to build and sell their machines in France. Wilbur's return to America in May 1909 was the occasion of widespread celebration. The brothers had become heroes.[25]

A resumption of the army trials at Fort Myer in July resulted in a ten-mile round-trip flight by Orville at a speed of over forty-two miles an hour. Its requirements met and exceeded by the Wrights, the army agreed to buy one of their planes for thirty thousand dollars. Almost simultaneously, Louis Bleriot of France flew across the English Channel—a glorious demonstration of the onrushing maturity of the airplane. The American Wright Company was incorporated in New York in November 1909, with Wilbur as president and Orville as a vice-president. By early 1910 it was producing two machines a month.[26] The airplane had shed its reputation as merely a potential plaything for rich sportsmen.

Kill Devil Hill forms a faint and distant backdrop for this bleak Kitty Hawk landscape around the time of the Wright brothers' final North Carolina experiments.
Motored vehicles were just beginning to appear on the Outer Banks, where many
residents saw an airplane in flight before they saw their first automobile. There were
still no bridges between the mainland and the barrier islands in 1911. *Wright State
University.*

A Final Fling at Kitty Hawk

The Wrights continued to work on improvements in flying, notably a
means to achieve automatic flight. Orville went to work on a new glider
to test the brothers' latest ideas for keeping a machine flying straight and
level without the pilot's intervention. He also made arrangements, when
finished, for a visit with it to Kill Devil Hills in the fall of 1911.[27]

The brothers had been hearing for some time that all was not well at
their old camp. Adam Etheridge, their five-dollar-a-year caretaker, was
sending them reports of all manner of conflict between their wooden
structures and the natural elements. The "box with the [1902] machine
in it" had been by 1906 "broken in two places." By 1910 he could add
that the roof was "leaking some and will be bad before the summer is
over," though he could fix it if they wished. He hoped they would "come
down so we can see you fly some more. . . . I always look in the paper for
your work & am glad to see what you are dooing." A rumor that surfman
Bob Westcott had torn down part of their shed drew from the builders a
request that, if that were true, he should be asked to "replace it at once."[28]

In March 1911, and again in April, Etheridge wrote to acknowledge
receipt of his annual retainer and to inform the brothers that he had
bought a roll of tar paper and repaired the roof of the camp building.

Unfortunately, a storm only in recent days had torn off a larger part ("half the length of the house") than was fixed. There were now "leaks in sevrel places all over the roof, . . . some places in the floar croased up whare it has leaked on it," and other damage. He would patch or repaper the roof as they chose.[29]

Orville reached Kitty Hawk on October 10, preceded by Lorin, who arrived on September 23. As Etheridge had implied, the camp was again—as in 1908—"a shambles." Pieces of the 1908 machine were poking from the sand, too damaged by weather and field mice to be of any use. Years later Margaret Hollowell of Elizabeth City recalled a Nags Head vacation in June 1908 when Edenton's Dossey Pruden and other boys visited the camp. They brought back relics, "mostly mechanical (including the launching cradle), with the report that the shed had been torn open, and everything was scattered about." Margaret and a company of girls went there, finding that "things were indeed in confusion" and the building wrecked. Someone, she added, "needing boards for some building had started stripping away the walls. There had been heavy winds, and papers were scattered everywhere."[30]

She gathered the papers, including a "fragment that looked like a telegram." There were initialed rifle targets (Orville's had a bull's-eye hit), "drawings of airplanes, sketches that looked like engineer's plans. . . ." She also "selected some fragments of the glider wings and tore off a flapping section of cloth." These treasures she stored in a shoe box at her family's Nags Head cottage, where they remained until she took them down in 1926. "Time and mice" had devoured most of the paper; but she sent the scraps to Orville Wright, who later returned them with a letter identifying those he recognized. Her more substantial relics, including "pieces of wood, painted a dull silver color," were sent to Orville, at his request, in 1947 when he was supervising reconstruction of the 1905 machine.[31]

The building itself, having been repaired by Adam Etheridge, could be used at once. While waiting for crates containing the new glider, Orville and his team of assistants, including brother Lorin, amused themselves with some oceanfront kite flying, fishing, and motorboat rides on the sound. The glider reached Kitty Hawk on the *Van Dusen* on October 13, and Orville went up in it three days later. Once more the arrival of the machine attracted a steady flow of visitors, including Bill Tate and his family and George Baum. There were also squads of reporters who poked around daily, took pictures, and solicited interviews.[32]

Finding the new glider ungainly, Orville made some changes by using pieces of the 1908 machine. On the afternoon of October 24 he was able to remain in the air for an incredible nine minutes and forty-five seconds. It was a world's record for gliding that would not be broken for another

In 1911 Orville returned to Kitty Hawk to experiment with a new glider developed to achieve automatic stability. Wilbur, absorbed by the brothers' burgeoning airplane manufacturing business and patent infringements, could not make the trip. In these two photographs by journalist Van Ness Harwood, Orville tests the glider before appreciative Bankers. *Courtesy of the State Archives, North Carolina Division of Archives and History, Raleigh.*

decade—the first instance of true soaring in flight. The Wrights had at last achieved what large birds had inspired them to duplicate in the 1890s.

On one occasion eight-year-old Lewis Tate, Bill's younger son, became the second member of his family to ride a glider, the Wrights each holding up a wing to accommodate him. The plane, "with Lewis holding on for dear life, rose to arm's length above their head," as his brother Elijah saw it, "and everyone could see that it was the force of the wind, and not the Wrights, that was holding it up." After two more days of flying, the camp broke up and Orville headed home. Elizabeth City's *Tar Heel*, acknowledging that the town had given but slight attention to the Wrights as recently as 1905, remarked that now they were "the cynosure of all eyes." (A year later, when aviator Bob Fowler performed some flights at the Albemarle Fair, Elizabeth City's *Weekly Advance* declared that it was the "first time an air ship has been exhibited in Eastern North Carolina.")[33]

The Lighthouse Man

This proved to be the end of a remarkable era in human history. Contracting typhoid fever, Wilbur died at home in Dayton on the morning of May 30, 1912. In November Adam Etheridge wrote Lorin with condolences on the passing of his brother and a pressing invitation for him and Orville to come back to Kitty Hawk: "I have thought of you all so many times since you left here. . . . would be glad to see you all come down again. doan't you expect to come down again to see us & fly some arond Kill Devil Hill again? we have not had such an excitement since you all left."[34] But the Wrights had done their last flying on the Outer Banks.

On learning of Wilbur's death, Bill Tate wrote to the state Hall of History in Raleigh about erecting a memorial to the brothers on the site in his front yard where Wilbur assembled the 1900 glider. To a friend he wrote that "[i]f Wilbur Wright had begun the assembly of that first experimental glider . . . on the front yard of some citizen in California . . . tons of printers ink would have been spread over the event, a monument would have marked the spot, and tourists would have come from thosands of miles, just to see and stand on the spot." Unhappily, even Bill's Kitty Hawk neighbors were cool to the idea, some supposing that he wanted the marker in order to enhance the value of his property. Only after selling the place years later would he renew his campaign.[35]

Apparently Bill Tate's correspondence with the Wrights lapsed for some years after 1909. He was now an active member of Currituck's Board of Education (for a while its chairman) and a Democrat earnest enough to be touted in 1910 for the state legislature. In July 1915 he joined the

United States Bureau of Lighthouses and was appointed keeper of the Long Point light at Coinjock, on the Currituck mainland. In the following year Orville sold his interest in the American Wright Company, thereafter going into technical retirement, though he remained professionally active as an aviation consultant.[36]

When Bill Tate finally wrote again to Orville in March 1922, it was to report that he and his family had remained faithful to the cause of aviation. Daughter Irene had married a professional aviator, Bennett D. Severn of New Jersey, and had flown more than ten thousand miles (she was the first woman to fly round trip between New York and Miami); son Elijah was a mechanic with Glenn H. Curtiss's airplane company. Lena had wed Elmer R. Woodard of the Imperial Tobacco Company of Great Britain and Ireland, and Lewis would soon graduate from business college. Orville replied that he was "deeply interested in the news of your children" and hoped "to again visit our old camps at Kitty Hawk, and to see you."[37]

Irene Tate's storybook romance had been one to please the heart of anyone associated with aviation. Bennett Severn had been flying his airplane from Atlantic City, New Jersey, to Florida in 1917 when he landed at Knotts Island near Bill Tate's Long Point Lighthouse in Currituck County. Severn there met Irene, known as "a remarkably pretty woman," and the two were wed in April 1918.[38]

In 1926 North Carolina's First District congressman, Lindsay Warren, conceived the idea of a federal monument to the Wright brothers at Kill Devil Hill. When his bill for that purpose was introduced into the House of Representatives on February 8, 1927, it passed that same day with an appropriation of $225,000 for the purpose. A contract to "anchor" wandering Big Hill (by then three-eighths of a mile from its 1903 location) by planting it with grass and shrubbery was awarded to Jesse Baum, who as a boy had been a frequent visitor to the Wright camp.[39]

The memorial project reawakened the slumbering correspondence of Bill Tate and Orville Wright. In 1926 Bill wrote Orville in some disdain that the town of Manteo, recently awakened to its peripheral role in the Wright experiments, now wished "to make it appear . . . that Manteo pretty near discovered the flight themselves, but I remember that it only woke up and took notice after the first flight was made, and they began to get a little income from the Metropolitian reporters who were attracted here."[40]

Not to be outdone, Kitty Hawk's citizens finally agreed on the idea that Tate had first suggested in 1912, a memorial in his old front yard. A commemorative five-foot marble obelisk was paid for by Kitty Hawk citizens (no others being allowed to contribute toward the $210 cost), including some three hundred schoolchildren. This first American monument to the Wright brothers was unveiled by Lena's son, Elmer R.

Bill Tate's daughter Irene around the time of her marriage to Bennett Severn in 1918. As a three-year-old in 1900, she wore a dress her mother, Addie Tate, made of sateen wing cloth from the first Wright glider. Irene became an avid aviator after her marriage. *Courtesy of her daughter, Willa Severn Raye.*

Woodard, Jr., in 1928. Speakers for the occasion included Bill Tate and the Reverend W. A. Betts. Bill was sure, he wrote Orville, that his family had "put more faith in your experiments and the outcome of success than any other North Carolinians." He told a reporter in 1932 that "I felt as close if not closer to them than any man in North Carolina in those days long ago."[41]

Should Orville come to the Outer Banks, Bill promised that he would find a different world from that of 1900. A bridge was soon to be built across Currituck Sound to Kitty Hawk, another from Manteo to Nags Head. Bill could now drive his own Willys-Knight from Norfolk to the tip of Powells Point in Currituck in a mere ninety minutes on "good concrete & dirt roads." Pending construction of the bridge, a ferry ran between Elizabeth City and Kitty Hawk in only half an hour. It was a far cry from the days of Israel Perry's washtub. A land developer in New Jersey had bought all the vacant land from Kitty Hawk to Hatteras and was laying off lots and streets for "the Virginia Dare Shores."[42]

Alive to the growing national interest in the work of the Wrights, Bill Tate and Elijah Baum had lately paid a visit to the Kill Devil Hill campsite. Scattered about in the sands were pieces of tar paper, the remains of two-by-fours the Wrights had driven into the sand, and other odds and ends from the work of a quarter century before. Gathering the relics into a pile, Bill had a photo made with himself and Elijah standing with the debris. He also compiled a scrapbook of clippings, pictures, and other

Airman Bennett D. Severn (*left*) and his partner E. K. Jaquith show off wildfowl
killed on a hunting expedition, probably in Currituck County in early January 1917.
The two owned this Curtiss Model F seaplane and toured coastal recreation areas
selling rides in it. Bennett landed at Knotts Island, near Bill Tate's Long Point Lighthouse, where he met and married Irene Tate. *Courtesy of Willa Severn Raye.*

memorabilia entitled "The Wright Brothers in Connection with Eastern
North Carolina."[43]

From this point until his own death in 1953, Bill Tate became a
leader—certainly the foremost one in North Carolina—among those who
championed the achievement of the Wright brothers and demanded that
the nation accord them full recognition. To him and many others across
the country, it was a source of acute embarrassment that the Smithsonian
Institution had never recognized the Wrights as the fathers of aviation,
insisting all along that its own Professor Langley deserved that title.
Smithsonian officers put forth the bizarre claim that Langley's plane,
despite its failures, was nonetheless capable of flight and therefore deserved
priority. They had even refused the Wrights' early offer of their 1903
Wright Flyer for the museum.[44]

Outraged by the Smithsonian's attitude, Orville in 1925 placed the
plane on loan with England's Science Museum in London. He vowed that
the historic aircraft would not come back to the United States unless the
Smithsonian renounced its position. The priceless machine would thus be
subjected to the German aerial blitz of World War II.[45]

In 1928 Bill Tate (*left*) and Elijah Baum visited the old Wright campsite at Kill Devil Hills and picked up these relics, presumably the remains of one or more of the buildings constructed there by the Wrights. *Wright State University.*

When ground was broken for the Wright Brothers National Memorial in December 1928, Bill Tate arranged to publish a twenty-fifth anniversary brochure of the first flight. It featured "data collected by Wm. J. Tate including some extracts from personal letters from Orville Wright" and other material he had gathered. The memorial, a sixty-foot Mount Airy granite pylon with gigantic wings carved in bas-relief, was completed and dedicated in November 1932. Orville and Bill were on hand at Big Hill dune for the occasion. In early December Bill, now head of the Kill Devil Hill Memorial Association, was invited to Washington as one of several speakers who paid tribute to the Wrights over NBC radio. His five-minute presentation was sliced to two, however, to make time for other accolades to be heard.[46]

Orville Wright (*left*) and Bill Tate. After 1903 Tate remained in frequent contact
with the Wrights for the rest of their lives. This picture was probably taken at the
dedication of the Wright Brothers National Memorial at Kill Devil Hills in 1932.
Wright State University.

In 1932, as head of the North Carolina branch of the National
Aeronautical Association, Tate threw his efforts into a campaign to force
the Smithsonian to recognize the Wrights' achievement and to persuade
Orville to allow the plane to come home. Speaking at a Wright Memorial
commemoration, he warned that the plane must be brought back during
Orville's lifetime "or it will never come. . . . It is a . . . humiliating condition
for Americans that . . . the greatest scientific discovery of the ages, although
born in the genius of two Americans, built and flown by Americans, is lost
to this nation forever. Think it over," he warned his countrymen, "and
bow your head in shame that you have done little about it."[47]

Bill Tate's efforts on the Wrights' behalf attracted wide attention. In 1938 Orville invited him and Adam Etheridge to attend the opening of a permanent exhibit at the Henry Ford Museum in Michigan featuring the reconstructed Wright homeplace and Dayton workshop. Bill was thrilled at the chance to meet Edsel and Henry Ford, and he enjoyed a two-minute conversation with the latter. His flight aboard Penn Central Airline from Norfolk, he informed Orville, was his twenty-second. In 1939 North Carolina governor Clyde R. Hoey appointed Tate to the seven-member North Carolina Aviation Committee, charged with studying aviation laws and recommending legislation to the state General Assembly. He was invited to Washington in the same year as a guest of the Aero Club, staying at the Shoreham Hotel.[48]

The reluctant Smithsonian finally conceded in 1942, and Orville thereafter altered his will to require that the Wright Flyer be lodged permanently at the institution at the war's conclusion. On December 17, 1948, the plane was officially presented to the public at the Smithsonian's Arts and Industries Building. Today it hangs from the ceiling of the

Bill Tate and his daughter Pauline (Lena) Tate Woodard at a commemoration of the first flight at Kitty Hawk. *Wright State University.*

National Air and Space Museum, the feature attraction among numerous flying machines. The unveiling was witnessed by Colington Island's Johnny Moore, who had helped launch the plane forty-five years earlier. Puzzled that Moore appeared only to glance momentarily at the plane, reporters drew from him the explanation "I seen it before."[49]

Bill Tate's correspondence with Orville continued after Tate's retirement from government service in 1940. In 1942 he noted that he was serving as chairman of Currituck County's Draft Board Number One. He updated Orville on the progress of his children (Lewis was aboard a naval vessel in the South Pacific) and grandchildren. He was pleased with Orville's gift in 1943 of Fred C. Kelly's authorized biography, *The Wright Brothers*. Many of Bill's letters to Dayton contained news stories about the Wrights from the Elizabeth City and other papers, some of which Bill corrected in letters to the editors. Orville, nearing the end, suffered a heart attack on October 10, 1947, and was hospitalized for four days.[50]

Passing the Torch

Orville's final letters from Bill Tate were those of October 13 and 30, 1947; one of the last letters written by Orville was his response to these missives. He told his old friend that he had "been hoping to make another trip to Kitty Hawk. . . , but this heart attack put a crimp in such plans." He was feeling better and hoped Addie's health, recently poor, was also improved. "We are all," he wrote, "older than we were 40 years ago when we saw most of each other. . . . I always read your letters with delight. Please write without waiting for letters from me." Orville's death on the evening of January 30, 1948, at age seventy-seven, brought the correspondence of almost half a century to a close. Bill was an honorary pallbearer at Orville's funeral.[51]

Within twenty-three hours after Orville's passing, John T. Daniels, whose snapshot of the first flight had become a classic in the annals of photography, also was dead. He had been stricken at the first-flight commemoration exercises on December 17. For many years he had served as operator of a ferry between Morehead City and Beaufort, where Elizabeth City newsman W. O. Saunders found him in 1927, "a rugged, bronzed, gray-haired, gray-eyed son of Neptune."[52]

Gradually the other principal figures in the Wrights' Outer Banks sojourns disappeared from the scene. Two preceded Daniels in death: W. Cephas (Ceef) Brinkley, a Manteo dairy farmer in his later years, and Adam Dough Etheridge in 1940. In September 1937 Etheridge and John T. Daniels had finally made their first flight aboard the invention they helped launch in 1903. They flew to the national air races in Cleveland, Ohio, as guests of the Early Birds, a society of old-time aviators. "When the invitation came," said Daniels, "and they said we could come by flying machine, we talked things over and decided we'd not chance it. We said we'd stick to the bus or train." But the pair "got to thinking it over" and had a change of heart. "We got into the flying machine at Norfolk, and . . . do you know it was the most pleasant ride we ever had. Why, when we got about to Pittsburgh, I went sound asleep." Bill Tate wrote Orville that he "just ought to hear the boys tell about the trip and what they saw."[53]

Johnny Moore remained for many years a primitive but colorful fishing and hunting guide at his Colington Island home. One well-known story about him concerned his work as a carpenter with Charles A. Spruill on the Nags Header hotel. Seeing a nail sticking out of a floor, Johnny bent it over with his bare heel. When Spruill asked how he did such a thing, Johnny explained that his feet were tough because he never washed them. Spruill inquired how the mother of his fourteen children felt about that, and Johnny replied that he tied bags over his feet when he went to bed. In later years his health deteriorated. On February 28, 1952, Johnny, the last surviving participant in the first flight, "blew his head off with a 12-gauge shotgun."[54]

The Wrights' official biographer, Fred C. Kelly, continued to correspond with Bill Tate, seeking new details of the glider experiments and first flight. The responses were always gracious and informative. Bill Tate, former member of the National Aeronautical Association, "first lighthouse employee to inspect aids to navigation by airplane" (according to his business card), died on June 8, 1953, at age eighty-three; his wife, Addie, died two years later, having survived a serious Outer Banks automobile accident in 1931.[55]

Tom Tate, the aeronaut of 1900, found employment in his later years as a farmhand, fisherman, huntsman, fishing guide, and mail carrier. He married Hannah Scarborough in 1913 and settled in the hamlet of Duck, eight miles north of Kitty Hawk. Tom gained a reputation as an indefatigable fishing guide. On one occasion a wave sat him down hard on a fishing plug on his boat seat. After several attempts by companions failed to dislodge the hooks with a knife, Tom declared, "Hell, let it go, we've got more fish to catch." Later in the day, at Caffeys Inlet, the hooks were removed with a razor and Tom immediately went back to his boat. He died at age sixty-eight in 1956 leaving his two children, Etta Elizabeth and Daniel Grady Tate.[56]

In 1967 Bill Tate's elder son, Elijah W. Tate of Coinjock, bought the sixty-five-foot sailboat *Hattie Creef*, which had once carried the Wrights and their machines to and from Kitty Hawk, from an Elizabeth City owner. He had the boat overhauled and rebuilt to serve as a Wright brothers museum. Its collection included Addie Tate's sewing machine,

Tom and Hannah Scarborough Tate's wedding picture, March 10, 1913,
Pasquotank County. They became the parents of Etta Elizabeth and Daniel Grady
Tate. Tom remained a lifelong fisherman and hunter. *Courtesy of Iva Tate Jordan,
their niece.*

numerous letters from Orville to Bill Tate, and other memorabilia. The
Hattie Creef ended its days ignominiously as a beach-front restaurant
before it was torn down. Its mementos became part of the collection at
the federal museum at the Wright Memorial.[57]

The widespread perception that the Wrights carried off their great
undertaking as two lonely figures amid scornful primitives is altogether
untrue and unjust. Apart from the scores of coastal North Carolinians

mentioned in the preceding pages, a great many other Tar Heels had a hand, directly or indirectly, in the work of the Wright brothers. They included Elizabeth City and Manteo merchants and millers, boat crewmen and surfmen, residents of the Kitty Hawk and Nags Head Woods communities, and others. None is recorded as having sought in any way to discourage or obstruct the Wrights.

It was a benign destiny that brought the Wright brothers to Kitty Hawk in the autumn of 1900. Had they chosen another destination, the advent of the airplane might have had to wait for years and the credit for it might well have gone to some other nation.

Notes

Chapter One

1. William J. Tate, "With the Wrights at Kitty Hawk," *Aeronautic Review* 6 (December 1928): 192.

2. Marvin W. McFarland, ed., *The Papers of Wilbur and Orville Wright*, 2 vols. (New York: McGraw-Hill Book Co., 1953), 2:33.

3. Tom D. Crouch, *The Eagle Aloft: Two Centuries of the Balloon in America* (Washington: Smithsonian Institution Press, 1983), passim; *Virginia Chronicle* (Norfolk), May 5, 1794.

4. *News and Observer* (Raleigh), October 19, 1888, October 16, 1890, October 25, 1900; *Tar Heel* (Elizabeth City), October 24, 1903.

5. Dennis Rogers, "Boy's Contraption Could Fly But Nobody Cared," *News and Observer*, November 10, 1978; James H. Gradeless, telephone interview with author, March 7, 1993.

6. F. Roy Johnson and E. Frank Stephenson, *The Gatling Gun and the Flying Machine* (Murfreesboro, N.C.: Johnson Publishing Co., 1979), passim; *Daily News* (Raleigh), May 2, 1872; *Norfolk Journal*, March 18, 1873.

7. Johnson and Stephenson, *Gatling Gun and Flying Machine*, 32-33, 128-134; Paul Wahl and Don Toppel, *The Gatling Gun* (New York: Arco Publishing Co., 1965), passim.

8. *Daily Charlotte Observer*, March 30, 1881; *Charlotte Observer*, October 6, 1929.

9. *Daily Charlotte Observer*, March 30, 1881, March 18, 1882; unidentified clipping in CA-741000-011, Documents on Daniel Asbury, National Air and Space Museum Library, Washington, D.C.

10. *Tar Heel*, October 24, 1902.

11. Hendrick De Leeuw, *Conquest of the Air: The History and Future of Aviation* (New York: Vantage Press, 1960), 69; Martin Grosser, *Gossamer Odyssey: The Triumph of Human-Powered Flight* (Boston: Houghton Mifflin Co., 1981).

12. Robert E. Ireland, *Entering the Auto Age: The Early Automobile in North Carolina* (Raleigh: Division of Archives and History, North Carolina Department of Cultural Resources, 1990), 1-28.

13. *Webster's Weekly* (Reidsville), May 1, 8, 1902; *Winston-Salem Journal*, May 17, 1902. Observations as to the system of flight used on Hill's dirigible were formed by the author from a photograph of the machine in his possession. The author's forthcoming book, tentatively entitled "Tar Heel Aeronauts before the Wright Brothers," will contain a reproduction of the photo.

14. *Union Republican* (Winston), June 27, 1902; *Charlotte Observer*, May 17, 1903; *Semi-Weekly Review* (Reidsville), February 18, 1902; *Virginian-Pilot* (Norfolk), December 19, 1903.

15. Ireland, *Entering the Auto Age*, 6-8.

16. *Semi-Weekly Review*, February 25, 1902; Donald Kromm, son of Louis H. Kromm, telephone interview with author, June 24, 1992.

17. Sister M. Virgina Geiger, *Daniel Carroll II: One Man and His Descendants, 1730-1978* (Baltimore: Schneidereith and Sons, 1979), 123; Lizzie Wilson Montgomery, *Sketches of Old Warrenton, North Carolina* (Raleigh: Edwards and Broughton Printing Co., 1924), 220-221; *Dictionary of North Carolina Biography*, s.v. "Christmas, William." See also Harry Combs, *Kill Devil Hill: Discovering the Secret of the Wright Brothers* (Boston: Houghton Mifflin Co., 1979), 356.

18. William W. Christmas, "Allies Order New Cantilever Airplanes," *New York Times*, December 5, 1915; Myron W. Stearns, "The Flying Wing," *Popular Mechanics* 52 (August 1929): 134-135; J. D. Van Vliet, "The Inside Story of the 'Bullet,'" *Popular Aviation* 15 (July 1934): 21-22, 52.

19. Harold E. Morehouse, "William W. Christmas: Eastern Pioneer Aviator—Plane Builder—Inventor," typescript in CC-266000-01, Documents on William W. Christmas, National Air and Space Museum Library.

20. *New York Times*, August 27, 1922, April 15, 1960.

21. William H. Rhodes, *The Indian Gallows and Other Poems* (New York: S. Walker, 1846), passim.

22. Sam Moskovitz, "The Science Fiction Hoaxes of William Henry Rhodes," introduction to *Caxton's Book: A Collection of Essays, Poems, Tales, and Sketches by the Late W. H. Rhodes*, ed. Daniel O'Connell (Westport, Ct.: Hyperion Press, 1974), [iv-v].

23. *Charlotte Observer*, November 25, 1901, January 27, 31, August 4, 14, 25, 1902.

24. *Charlotte Observer*, May 10, August 31, December 11, 1903.

25. *Wilmington Messenger*, April 6, 1897; *News and Observer*, April 13, 16, 1897; *Fayetteville Observer*, April 10, 1897; *Sanford Express*, April 16, 1897.

26. David M. Jacobs, *The UFO Controversy in America* (Bloomington: Indiana University Press, 1975), 10-30.

27. Ben Mackworth-Praed, ed., *Aviation: The Pioneer Years* (Secaucus, N.J.: Chartwell Books, 1990), 82; Richard Walser, "Jules Verne's Fantastic Voyage to North Carolina," *State* 55 (December 1987): 32-33; *Tar Heel*, October 24, 1902.

Chapter Two

1. Fred C. Kelly, *The Wright Brothers* (New York: Harcourt, Brace and Co., 1943), 1, 22-23.

2. Tom D. Crouch, *The Bishop's Boys: A Life of Wilbur and Orville Wright* (New York: W. W. Norton and Co., 1989), 54-170.

3. Crouch, *Bishop's Boys*, 32-35.

4. Kelly, *Wright Brothers*, 22-27; Catherine Albertson, *Wings over Kill Devil Hill and Legends of the Dunes* (n.p., n.d.), 13. Pp. 3-18 of the latter source reprint

a portion of W. J. Tate, *Brochure of the Twenty-fifth Anniversary of the First Successful Airplane Flight, 1903-1928: Kitty Hawk, N.C., December 17, 1928* (Kitty Hawk: the author, 1928). The brochure was issued by Tate at the twenty-fifth anniversary of the first flight and presented to members of the International Air Congress who visited Kill Devil Hill on December 17, 1928.

5. Kelly, *Wright Brothers*, 25-27; Albertson, *Wings over Kill Devil Hill*, 13.

6. Kelly, *Wright Brothers*, 29-30.

7. Combs, *Kill Devil Hill*, 34-37.

8. Crouch, *Bishop's Boys*, 94-96.

9. John E. Walsh, *One Day at Kitty Hawk: The Untold Story of the Wright Brothers and the Airplane* (New York: Thomas Y. Crowell Co., 1975), 10-17.

10. Walsh, *One Day at Kitty Hawk*, 11-13.

11. Crouch, *Bishop's Boys*, 51-82.

12. Crouch, *Bishop's Boys*, 96-101; Albertson, *Wings over Kill Devil Hill*, 14.

13. Crouch, *Bishop's Boys*, 101-111; Albertson, *Wings over Kill Devil Hill*, 14.

14. Kelly, *Wright Brothers*, 38-44.

15. Kelly, *Wright Brothers*, 39-43.

16. Kelly, *Wright Brothers*, 39-43.

17. Kelly, *Wright Brothers*, 44.

18. Crouch, *Bishop's Boys*, 14-15; Walsh, *One Day at Kitty Hawk*, 12-17.

19. Walsh, *One Day at Kitty Hawk*, 16; W. O. Saunders, "Then We Quit Laughing," *Independent* (Elizabeth City), November 18, 1932. This article first appeared in *Collier's* 80 (September 17, 1927).

20. Kelly, *Wright Brothers*, 5-8.

21. Kelly, *Wright Brothers*, 12; Crouch, *Bishop's Boys*, 57, 159; James Farber, "Orville Wright Interviewed," *Popular Aviation* 14 (April 1934): 224.

22. Walsh, *One Day at Kitty Hawk*, 18-19.

23. Walsh, *One Day at Kitty Hawk*, 23.

24. Crouch, *Bishop's Boys*, 142-144.

25. Walsh, *One Day at Kitty Hawk*, 2-3, 6-9, 24-25, 45-48; Combs, *Kill Devil Hill*, 25, 40.

26. Crouch, *Bishop's Boys*, 160-161.

27. Kelly, *Wright Brothers*, 46-48.

28. Crouch, *Bishop's Boys*, 166.

29. Combs, *Kill Devil Hill*, 63-68; Crouch, *Bishop's Boys*, 137.

30. Walsh, *One Day at Kitty Hawk*, 33.

31. Walsh, *One Day at Kitty Hawk*, 21-31.

32. Combs, *Kill Devil Hill*, 187.

33. Crouch, *Bishop's Boys*, 138-142, 256-258.

34. Walsh, *One Day at Kitty Hawk*, 36-37.

35. Kelly, *Wright Brothers*, 49-50.

36. Crouch, *Bishop's Boys*, 173-174.

37. Kelly, *Wright Brothers*, 57.

38. McFarland, *Papers of Wilbur and Orville Wright* 1:23; Crouch, *Bishop's Boys*, 181-182.

39. Kelly, *Wright Brothers*, 55-56; Tate, "With the Wrights at Kitty Hawk," 191; *Morning Herald* (Durham), May 10, 1970; Albertson, *Wings over Kill Devil Hill*, 12.

40. Crouch, *Bishop's Boys*, 182-183.

41. Combs, *Kill Devil Hill*, 82-83; Albertson, *Wings over Kill Devil Hill*, 3.

42. Combs, *Kill Devil Hill*, 82-83; W. J. Tate to Wilbur Wright, August 18, 1900, General Correspondence, Papers of Wilbur and Orville Wright, Manuscript Division, Library of Congress, Washington, D.C.

43. Combs, *Kill Devil Hill*, 82-83.

44. Combs, *Kill Devil Hill*, 83; Catherine W. Bishir, "The 'Unpainted Aristocracy': The Beach Cottages of Old Nags Head," *North Carolina Historical Review* 54 (October 1977): 381.

45. Luis Marden, "She Wore the World's First Wings," *Outer Banks Magazine*, 1984, 25. This article's author was evidently permitted to examine W. J. Tate's papers, then in the possession of Tate's daughter, Mrs. Elmer R. (Lena) Woodard of Coinjock.

46. Crouch, *Bishop's Boys*, 183-184.

Chapter Three

1. Crouch, *Bishop's Boys*, 183.

2. Crouch, *Bishop's Boys*, 184.

3. Crouch, *Bishop's Boys*, 184; McFarland, *Papers of Wilbur and Orville Wright* 1:32; *Coastland Times* (Manteo), December 11, 1953.

4. Kelly, *Wright Brothers*, 58-59.

5. McFarland, *Papers of Wilbur and Orville Wright* 1:24-25.

6. McFarland, *Papers of Wilbur and Orville Wright* 1:24-25.

7. McFarland, *Papers of Wilbur and Orville Wright* 1:25.

8. Kelly, *Wright Brothers*, 59.

9. McFarland, *Papers of Wilbur and Orville Wright* 1:33; W. J. Tate to Wilbur and Orville Wright, November 2, 1900, Wright Papers.

10. McFarland, *Papers of Wilbur and Orville Wright* 1:25; Elizabeth Baum Hanbury, *Currituck Legacy: The Baum Family of North Carolina* (n.p. 1985), 85-86; *Citizen-Times* (Asheville), October 18, 1953; *Coastland Times*, December 11, 1953; Tate, "With the Wrights at Kitty Hawk," 191; W. J. Tate to Orville Wright, September 21, 1927, Wright Papers.

11. Tate, "With the Wrights at Kitty Hawk," 191.

12. McFarland, *Papers of Wilbur and Orville Wright* 1:25, 33; Tate, "With the Wrights at Kitty Hawk," 191.

13. Crouch, *Bishop's Boys*, 187; Tate, "With the Wrights at Kitty Hawk," 191; Marden, "She Wore the World's First Wings," 27.

14. Marden, "She Wore the World's First Wings," 27.

15. Tate, "With the Wrights at Kitty Hawk," 191; McFarland, *Papers of Wilbur and Orville Wright* 1:25; Crouch, *Bishop's Boys*, 187.

16. W. J. Tate to Orville Wright, May 6, 1928, Wright Papers.

17. McFarland, *Papers of Wilbur and Orville Wright* 1:25-26; David Stick, *Dare County: A History* (Raleigh: Division of Archives and History, North Carolina Department of Cultural Resources, 1970), 18.

18. McFarland, *Papers of Wilbur and Orville Wright* 1:25; Works Progress Administration, *Who's Who in Aviation: A Directory of Living Men and Women Who Have Contributed to the Growth of Aviation in the United States* (Chicago: Ziff-Davis Publishing Co., 1942), 423; Daniel Grady Tate, "William James Tate" and "W. J. Tate and Family," in *The Heritage of Currituck County, North Carolina*, ed. Jo Anne Bates (Winston-Salem: Hunter Publishing Co., 1985), 419-420. D. G. Tate is a grandson of Dan Tate, who was a half brother of W. J. Tate.

19. Tate, "William James Tate," 419; D. G. Tate, "Daniel M. Tate," in *Heritage of Currituck County*, 417; Twelfth Census of the United States, 1900: Currituck County, North Carolina, Population Schedule, National Archives, Washington, D.C.; *Tar Heel*, April 4, 1902.

20. Tate, "W. J. Tate and Family," 420.

21. Stick, *Dare County*, 17-18; Saunders, "Then We Quit Laughing."

22. McFarland, *Papers of Wilbur and Orville Wright* 1:26; Hilda Scull, "Kitty Hawk Revisited," *Coastlander* (Manteo), May 1973. The latter source includes reminiscences of Truxton Midgett and Jesse Baum.

23. Stick, *Dare County*, 43-46; Scull, "Kitty Hawk Revisited."

24. Stick, *Dare County*, 44-45; L. D. Hayman, "The Fish Camp Colony: Shad Fishing in Dare County Waters Fifty Years Ago," *Coastland Times*, March 9, 1956.

25. McFarland, *Papers of Wilbur and Orville Wright* 1:31-33; Scull, "Kitty Hawk Revisited."

26. Crouch, *Bishop's Boys*, 194; Twelfth Census, 1900: Currituck County Population Schedule.

27. Stick, *Dare County*, 28-29; Donald McAdoo and Carol McAdoo, *Reflections of the Outer Banks* (Manteo: Island Publishing House, 1976), 89.

28. Saunders, "Then We Quit Laughing"; McAdoo and McAdoo, *Reflections of the Outer Banks*, 31. The remarks on the Wrights are those of Mrs. Lillie Etheridge Swindell, who married, first, Adam D. Etheridge.

29. Scull, "Kitty Hawk Revisited"; Crouch, *Bishop's Boys*, 191; McFarland, *Papers of Wilbur and Orville Wright* 1:33, 371.

30. Twelfth Census, 1900: Currituck County Population Schedule. Dr. Cogswell is listed as a Connecticut native. Wilbur Wright thought he was from New York, perhaps Cogswell's last place of residence. He had married in 1896 and had a three-year-old son, William L. (Wink) Cogswell. See D. G. Tate, "Thomas Douglas Tate," in *Heritage of Currituck County*, 418. Kitty Hawk became part of Dare County in 1920. See Stick, *Dare County*, 34; McFarland, *Papers of Wilbur and Orville Wright* 1:39.

31. Twelfth Census, 1900: Currituck County Population Schedule; Crouch, *Bishop's Boys*, 191; Mrs. Iva Tate Jordan, interview with author, February 19, 1993.

32. Bishir, "Unpainted Aristocracy"; *Tar Heel*, July 31, 1903.

33. Bishir, "Unpainted Aristocracy," 380; Edward R. Outlaw, Jr., and Louise Greenleaf Outlaw, *Old Nag's Head* (Norfolk, Va.: Liskey Lithograph Corp.,

108

1956), 36-37; Bill Sharpe, "An Unknown Celebrity," *State* 15 (March 3, 1948): 7.

34. Stick, *Dare County*, passim.

35. Kelly, *Wright Brothers*, 63; Crouch, *Bishop's Boys*, 187.

36. McFarland, *Papers of Wilbur and Orville Wright* 1:26; Marden, "She Wore the World's First Wings," 23; Crouch, *Bishop's Boys*, 187; *News and Observer*, December 10, 1967, September 17, 1979.

37. Crouch, *Bishop's Boys*, 188; McFarland, *Papers of Wilbur and Orville Wright* 1:29-30.

38. W. J. Tate to Fred C. Kelly, October 28, 1951, Wright Papers.

39. Kelly, *Wright Brothers*, 63.

40. McFarland, *Papers of Wilbur and Orville Wright* 1:31-33; W. J. Tate to Fred C. Kelly, December 5, 1951, Wright Papers.

41. McFarland, *Papers of Wilbur and Orville Wright* 1:33.

42. W. J. Tate to Fred C. Kelly, October 28, 1951, Wright Papers; McFarland, *Papers of Wilbur and Orville Wright* 1:31.

43. Crouch, *Bishop's Boys*, 188-190.

44. McFarland, *Papers of Wilbur and Orville Wright* 1:29-39.

45. Crouch, *Bishop's Boys*, 185-190; *Eden News*, December 18, 1970.

46. Crouch, *Bishop's Boys*, 190-191.

47. Kelly, *Wright Brothers*, 63-64.

48. McFarland, *Papers of Wilbur and Orville Wright* 1:29, 33. Bill Tate's letters to the Wrights use the terms "Mr. Wilbur" and "Mr. Orville."

49. W. O. Saunders, "Then We Quit Laughing"; Adam D. Etheridge IV, son of Adam T. Etheridge, interview with author, March 24, 1993; Mrs. Mellie Daniels Pearce, daughter of John T. Daniels, interview with author, February 19, 1993.

50. McFarland, *Papers of Wilbur and Orville Wright* 1:39-40. The Wrights wrote Cahoon's name incorrectly as Calhoun. He is listed as a merchant in the 1900 Atlantic Township census. See Twelfth Census, 1900: Currituck County Population Schedule.

51. *News and Observer*, December 15, 1943.

52. McFarland, *Papers of Wilbur and Orville Wright* 1:36, 39.

53. Crouch, *Bishop's Boys*, 191.

54. Crouch, *Bishop's Boys*, 196-197.

55. Crouch, *Bishop's Boys*, 196-198.

56. Crouch, *Bishop's Boys*, 199.

57. McFarland, *Papers of Wilbur and Orville Wright* 1:33.

58. Crouch, *Bishop's Boys*, 199; W. J. Tate to Wilbur and Orville Wright, November 2, 1900, Wright Papers; Marden, "She Wore the World's First Wings," 23; *News and Observer*, December 17, 1975; *Greensboro Daily News*, December 18, 1975.

59. W. J. Tate to Wilbur and Orville Wright, November 2, 1900, Wright Papers.

60. W. J. Tate to Wilbur and Orville Wright, November 2, 1900, Wright Papers; Albertson, *Wings over Kill Devil Hill*, 7-8.

61. For the Tate children, see Twelfth Census, 1900: Currituck County Population Schedule.

62. Marden, "She Wore the World's First Wings," 23; *News and Observer*, April 23, 1961, December 17, 1975; *Greensboro Daily News*, December 18, 1975.

63. *Greensboro Daily News*, December 18, 1975.

64. Marden, "She Wore the World's First Wings," 27.

Chapter Four

1. Crouch, *Bishop's Boys*, 203.

2. Crouch, *Bishop's Boys*, 203.

3. Crouch, *Bishop's Boys*, 205-206.

4. Crouch, *Bishop's Boys*, 202-203.

5. W. J. Tate to Wilbur Wright, February 8, March 17, 1901, Wright Papers.

6. W. J. Tate to Wilbur Wright, March 17, 1901, Wright Papers.

7. Crouch, *Bishop's Boys*, 207.

8. McFarland, *Papers of Wilbur and Orville Wright* 1:72.

9. McFarland, *Papers of Wilbur and Orville Wright* 1:68.

10. W. J. Tate to Wilbur Wright, April 29, June 9, June 30, July 5, 1901; Sharber and White to Wilbur Wright, June 27, 1901, all in Wright Papers.

11. McFarland, *Papers of Wilbur and Orville Wright* 1:72-75.

12. Saunders, "Then We Quit Laughing"; McAdoo and McAdoo, *Reflections of the Outer Banks*, 31.

13. Crouch, *Bishop's Boys*, 207-208; McFarland, *Papers of Wilbur and Orville Wright* 1:72-74.

14. Crouch, *Bishop's Boys*, 208-209; McFarland, *Papers of Wilbur and Orville Wright* 1:75-76.

15. Crouch, *Bishop's Boys*, 210-211.

16. Crouch, *Bishop's Boys*, 211.

17. Crouch, *Bishop's Boys*, 211.

18. Pearce interview; *Greensboro Daily News*, August 4, 1971.

19. Unidentified newspaper clipping in John C. Summerson, Jr., "The Albemarle Sound Region and the Outer Banks of North Carolina, 1738-1939," scrapbook in Sargeant Room, Kirn Library, Norfolk, Va.; McFarland, *Papers of Wilbur and Orville Wright* 1:82; *Economist* (Elizabeth City), June 19, 1903.

20. McFarland, *Papers of Wilbur and Orville Wright* 1:81; Crouch, *Bishop's Boys*, 212.

21. McFarland, *Papers of Wilbur and Orville Wright* 1:83-84; Crouch, *Bishop's Boys*, 212-213.

22. Walsh, *One Day at Kitty Hawk*, 79; Combs, *Kill Devil Hill*, 108; Crouch, *Bishop's Boys*, 213.

23. McFarland, *Papers of Wilbur and Orville Wright* 1:116-117.

24. W. J. Tate to Wilbur Wright, October 11, 1901, Wright Papers.

25. Crouch, *Bishop's Boys*, 220-241.

26. Crouch, *Bishop's Boys*, 226.

27. Walsh, *One Day at Kitty Hawk*, 97-98.

28. McFarland, *Papers of Wilbur and Orville Wright* 1:241, 254.

29. McFarland, *Papers of Wilbur and Orville Wright* 1:237-238.

30. *Union Republican*, June 27, 1902; *Semi-Weekly Review*, February 25, 1902.

31. McFarland, *Papers of Wilbur and Orville Wright* 1:241.

32. McFarland, *Papers of Wilbur and Orville Wright* 1:244-245. Franklin H. Midgett is listed in the 1900 Atlantic Township census as a thirty-eight-year-old surfman and farm owner with a wife, Mary H., and six children. See Twelfth Census, 1900: Currituck County Population Schedule. See also McAdoo and McAdoo, *Reflections of the Outer Banks*, 30.

33. F. K. Kramer, "Kramers: Ninety Years in the Lumber Business in Elizabeth City, North Carolina" (typescript, East Carolina Manuscript Collection, East Carolina University Library, Greenville, N.C.), 47.

34. McFarland, *Papers of Wilbur and Orville Wright* 1:245; *Greensboro Daily News*, August 4, 1971.

35. Crouch, *Bishop's Boys*, 236-237.

36. McFarland, *Papers of Wilbur and Orville Wright* 1:245; *Eden News*, December 18, 1970; Pearce interview.

37. Crouch, *Bishop's Boys*, 237; McFarland, *Papers of Wilbur and Orville Wright* 1:253.

38. Crouch, *Bishop's Boys*, 237; Marden, "She Wore the World's First Wings," 29.

39. McFarland, *Papers of Wilbur and Orville Wright* 1:281.

40. Crouch, *Bishop's Boys*, 238.

41. Crouch, *Bishop's Boys*, 239.

42. *Tar Heel*, October 3, 1902.

43. *Tar Heel*, October 3, 1902.

44. McFarland, *Papers of Wilbur and Orville Wright* 1:249, 250, 251, 254, 258, 260, 262, 270, 275, 276, 277; McAdoo and McAdoo, *Reflections of the Outer Banks*, 31; W. J. Tate to Fred C. Kelly, November 1, 1951, Wright Papers.

45. McFarland, *Papers of Wilbur and Orville Wright* 1:283; W. J. Tate to Wilbur Wright, undated (1902?), Wright Papers; *Tar Heel*, August 24, 1902. Tate informed Wilbur that the brothers could stay with either Cogswell or George Baum until they left for camp.

46. McFarland, *Papers of Wilbur and Orville Wright* 1:277, 280.

47. Crouch, *Bishop's Boys*, 240; Marden, "She Wore the World's First Wings," 29.

48. Saunders, "Then We Quit Laughing"; *Tar Heel*, October 17, 1902.

49. Tate, *Brochure of the Twenty-fifth Anniversary*, 3-4.

50. McFarland, *Papers of Wilbur and Orville Wright* 1:281-284.

51. McFarland, *Papers of Wilbur and Orville Wright* 1:284.

52. Crouch, *Bishop's Boys*, 242-252.

Chapter Five

1. Crouch, *Bishop's Boys*, 243-245.
2. Crouch, *Bishop's Boys*, 244-245.
3. Crouch, *Bishop's Boys*, 242-243.
4. Crouch, *Bishop's Boys*, 243.
5. Crouch, *Bishop's Boys*, 243-244.
6. Crouch, *Bishop's Boys*, 246, 255-256.
7. Crouch, *Bishop's Boys*, 253-254.
8. Crouch, *Bishop's Boys*, 255; W. J. Tate to Wilbur Wright, July 22, 1903, Wright Papers.
9. *Tar Heel*, July 9, August 14, 1903.
10. McFarland, *Papers of Wilbur and Orville Wright* 1:356.
11. McFarland, *Papers of Wilbur and Orville Wright* 1:356-357.
12. Outlaw and Outlaw, *Old Nag's Head*, 28, 45-46; *Economist*, July 31, 1903.
13. McFarland, *Papers of Wilbur and Orville Wright* 1:357, 374-375.
14. McFarland, *Papers of Wilbur and Orville Wright* 1:373-374.
15. McFarland, *Papers of Wilbur and Orville Wright* 1:357, 358, 361; *Economist*, September 18, 1903.
16. Crouch, *Bishop's Boys*, 257-258.
17. McFarland, *Papers of Wilbur and Orville Wright* 1:358, 359, 361, 363, 373, 374, 375, 377, 378.
18. Homer M. Keever, *Iredell: Piedmont County* (Statesville, N.C.: Brady Printing Co., 1975), 314-315; Tate, "With the Wrights at Kitty Hawk," 189.
19. Saunders, "Then We Quit Laughing."
20. Saunders, "Then We Quit Laughing."
21. McFarland, *Papers of Wilbur and Orville Wright* 1:365.
22. McFarland, *Papers of Wilbur and Orville Wright* 1:366-367; *Economist*, October 30, 1903.
23. *Economist*, October 16, 1903.
24. McFarland, *Papers of Wilbur and Orville Wright* 1:375; *Tar Heel*, October 17, 1902.
25. McFarland, *Papers of Wilbur and Orville Wright* 1:375; Jordan interview.
26. McFarland, *Papers of Wilbur and Orville Wright* 1:375-381.
27. Alpheus W. Drinkwater, "I *Knew* Those Wright Brothers Were Crazy," *Reader's Digest* 69 (November 1956): 188-189.
28. Drinkwater, "I *Knew* Those Wright Brothers Were Crazy," 189.
29. Saunders, "Then We Quit Laughing."
30. John T. Daniels, "Wrights' First Short Flight 'Something' to an Eyewitness," unidentified clipping, 1943, Clipping File, North Carolina Collection, University of North Carolina Library, Chapel Hill.
31. McFarland, *Papers of Wilbur and Orville Wright* 1:383.
32. McFarland, *Papers of Wilbur and Orville Wright* 1:371-384.
33. Drinkwater, "I *Knew* Those Wright Brothers Were Crazy," 189.
34. Drinkwater, "I *Knew* Those Wright Brothers Were Crazy," 189, 192.
35. *Virginian-Pilot*, December 9, 1903; Combs, *Kill Devil Hill*, 200.

36. Crouch, *Bishop's Boys*, 263-264; Saunders, "Then We Quit Laughing."

37. Walsh, *One Day at Kitty Hawk*, 135.

38. Crouch, *Bishop's Boys*, 264.

39. Crouch, *Bishop's Boys*, 264.

40. Crouch, *Bishop's Boys*, 265.

41. Walsh, *One Day at Kitty Hawk*, 139.

42. Crouch, *Bishop's Boys*, 265-266.

43. Crouch, *Bishop's Boys*, 266; Outlaw and Outlaw, *Old Nag's Head*, 49; Aycock Brown, *The Birth of Aviation: Kitty Hawk, N.C.* (Winston-Salem: Collins Co., 1953), [15]; Twelfth Census, 1900: Dare County, North Carolina, Population Schedule. The Manteo Town census contains data on John T. Daniels, William S. Dough, Adam D. Etheridge, and William C. Brinkley.

44. W. J. Tate to Wilbur Wright, December 26, 1903, Wright Papers; *Carolina Coast*, December 17, 1987.

45. Saunders, "Then We Quit Laughing."

46. Crouch, *Bishop's Boys*, 267.

47. Crouch, *Bishop's Boys*, 267; Saunders, "Then We Quit Laughing"; *Tar Heel*, October 3, 1902.

48. Crouch, *Bishop's Boys*, 267-268; Saunders, "Then We Quit Laughing."

49. Crouch, *Bishop's Boys*, 268.

50. Albertson, *Wings over Kill Devil Hill*, 9; Crouch, *Bishop's Boys*, 268; Mrs. Lois Daniels Smith, granddaughter of John T. Daniels, interview with author, March 3, 1993. Mrs. Smith owns the photograph sent by the Wrights to her grandfather.

51. Saunders, "Then We Quit Laughing."

52. Saunders, "Then We Quit Laughing."

53. Daniels, "Wrights' First Short Flight."

54. Hanbury, *Currituck Legacy*, 85-86; Clary Thompson, "First Flight Witness Was Bored," unidentified newspaper clipping in Clipping File, North Carolina Collection.

55. Daniels, "Wrights' First Short Flight"; Lawrence Maddrey, unidentified *Virginian-Pilot* newspaper article, clipping in possession of Mrs. Lois Daniels Smith.

56. McFarland, *Papers of Wilbur and Orville Wright* 1:394; "They Too Saw First Flight," *State* 17 (June 11, 1949): 11.

57. Harry P. Moore, "Lifesavers Gave Him Tip Minutes after Wright Brothers' First Flight, Reporter Says Forty-six Years Later," *Virginian-Pilot*, December 11, 1949.

58. Crouch, *Bishop's Boys*, 269; "Two Old Timers," *Popular Aviation* 21 (October 1937): 16.

59. Saunders, "Then We Quit Laughing."

60. Saunders, "Then We Quit Laughing"; diary of Wilbur Wright, December 23, 1903, Wright Papers; Angelo Maschio, "Daniels' Father Took Picture of First Flight," *Eden News*, December 18, 1975.

61. Crouch, *Bishop's Boys*, 270.

62. Crouch, *Bishop's Boys*, 269-270.

63. *News and Observer*, October 7, 1902; *Tar Heel*, October 3, 1902.

64. Ora L. Jones, "Florida Man Explains His Part with First Airplane Flight at Kitty Hawk," *Daily Advance* (Elizabeth City), December 17, 1948.

65. Jones, "Florida Man Explains."

66. Jones, "Florida Man Explains."

67. Moore, "Lifesavers Gave Him Tip."

68. Moore, "Lifesavers Gave Him Tip"; Robert Mason, "When Flying Was News," *Virginian-Pilot*, December 17, 1950.

69. Crouch, *Bishop's Boys*, 270.

70. McFarland, *Papers of Wilbur and Orville Wright* 1:397; Combs, *Kill Devil Hill*, 225.

71. Mason, "When Flying Was News."

72. Mason, "When Flying Was News."

73. Mason, "When Flying Was News"; Robert Mason, *One of the Neighbors' Kids* (Chapel Hill: Algonquin Books, 1987), 121-122.

74. *Virginian-Pilot*, December 19, 1903.

75. Crouch, *Bishop's Boys*, 271.

76. Crouch, *Bishop's Boys*, 272.

77. Aycock Brown, "Alpheus Drinkwater Gives Own Version of Sending Out First Message of Flight," *Daily Advance*, November 30, 1948.

78. Mason, *One of the Neighbors' Kids*, 121-122.

79. *News and Observer*, December 19, 1903; *Charlotte Observer*, May 17, 1903, reprinted from *Morning Star* (Wilmington); *Charlotte Observer*, December 25, 1903.

80. McFarland, *Papers of Wilbur and Orville Wright* 1:398-399.

81. *Virginian-Pilot*, December 22, 23, 24, 1903.

82. W. J. Tate to Wilbur Wright, December 26, 1903, Wright Papers.

Chapter Six

1. Crouch, *Bishop's Boys*, 273; W. J. Tate to Wilbur Wright, December 26, 1903, Wright Papers.

2. Crouch, *Bishop's Boys*, 274, 276.

3. Crouch, *Bishop's Boys*, 276, 300.

4. Crouch, *Bishop's Boys*, 273-286.

5. Crouch, *Bishop's Boys*, 289-300.

6. Crouch, *Bishop's Boys*, 300-311.

7. Crouch, *Bishop's Boys*, 313-326.

8. Stearns, "Flying Wing," 236.

9. W. J. Tate to Wilbur Wright, August 4, 1906, Wright Papers.

10. Unsigned typescript letter to A. D. Etheridge, September 23, 1909, Wright Papers.

11. W. J. Tate to Wilbur Wright, April 1, 1908, June 20, 1909, Wright Papers.

12. W. J. Tate to Wilbur Wright, April 1, 1908, Wright Papers.

13. Crouch, *Bishop's Boys*, 338, 346, 354; Combs, *Kill Devil Hill*, 258.

14. McFarland, *Papers of Wilbur and Orville Wright* 2:861; Kramer, "Kramers," 35.

15. McFarland, *Papers of Wilbur and Orville Wright* 2:862.

16. McFarland, *Papers of Wilbur and Orville Wright* 2:863-864.

17. McFarland, *Papers of Wilbur and Orville Wright* 2:863-865.

18. McFarland, *Papers of Wilbur and Orville Wright* 2:865-867.

19. Kramer, "Kramers," 47-48.

20. McFarland, *Papers of Wilbur and Orville Wright* 2:866-867.

21. Crouch, *Bishop's Boys*, 355-356.

22. Crouch, *Bishop's Boys*, 355-358.

23. Crouch, *Bishop's Boys*, 358-359; McFarland, *Papers of Wilbur and Orville Wright* 2:867-872, 880-881.

24. Crouch, *Bishop's Boys*, 347, 375-376.

25. Crouch, *Bishop's Boys*, 381-394.

26. Crouch, *Bishop's Boys*, 399, 410, 424.

27. Crouch, *Bishop's Boys*, 443-444.

28. A. D. Etheridge to Wright brothers, November 15, 1906, May 9, 1910, Wright Papers.

29. A. D. Etheridge to Wright brothers, March 10, April 7, August 15, 1911, Wright Papers.

30. Crouch, *Bishop's Boys*, 443; Ben Dixon MacNeill, *News and Observer* article, January 16, 1938, Clipping File, North Carolina Collection; *Tar Heel*, September 22, 1911.

31. *News and Observer*, January 16, 1938.

32. *News and Observer*, December 31, 1947.

33. McFarland, *Papers of Wilbur and Orville Wright* 2:1024-1025; Crouch, *Bishop's Boys*, 443-444; Marden, "She Wore the World's First Wings," 28-29; *Tar Heel*, October 13, 1911; *Weekly Advance* (Elizabeth City), October 11, 1912.

34. Crouch, *Bishop's Boys*, 449; A. D. Etheridge to Lorin Wright, November 12, 1912, Wright Papers.

35. Tate, "With the Wrights at Kitty Hawk," 192; W. J. Tate to Orville Wright, December 3, 1927, Wright Papers.

36. W. J. Tate to Orville Wright, July 1, 1940, Wright Papers; Crouch, *Bishop's Boys*, 468; *Tar Heel*, August 13, 1909, April 23, 1910.

37. W. J. Tate to Orville Wright, March 19, 1922, Wright Papers; Willa Severn Raye, daughter of Irene Tate Severn, telephone interview with author, September 4, 1993; *Daily Advance*, January 22, 1917.

38. Crouch, *Bishop's Boys*, 505; *Greensboro Daily News*, August 4, 1971; Fred A. Olds, "The Mother of the Airplane," *Orphan's Friend and Masonic Journal* (Oxford, N.C.), September 20, 1918.

39. W. J. Tate to Orville Wright, December 19, 1926, Wright Papers.

40. W. J. Tate to Orville Wright, December 19, 1926, Wright Papers.

41. W. J. Tate to Orville Wright, March 19, December 19, 1926, Wright Papers; Albertson, *Wings over Kill Devil Hill*, 16-17; Saunders, "Then We Quit Laughing."

42. W. J. Tate to Orville Wright, December 19, 1926, Wright Papers.

43. W. J. Tate to Orville Wright, April 24, 1927, December 15, 1935, Wright Papers; photo of Tate and Baum with relics in Summerson, "The Albemarle Sound Region."

44. Crouch, *Bishop's Boys*, 484-502, 519-521.

45. Crouch, *Bishop's Boys*, 487-491.

46. Albertson, *Wings over Kill Devil Hill*, passim; Crouch, *Bishop's Boys*, 506-507; W. J. Tate to Orville Wright, December 10, 18, 1933, Wright Papers.

47. *News and Observer*, December 18, 1940.

48. W. J. Tate to Orville Wright, May 15, 1938, March 20, 1939, Wright Papers.

49. Crouch, *Bishop's Boys*, 527; *News and Observer*, December 18, 1948.

50. W. J. Tate to Orville Wright, September 16, 1940, October 28, 1942, May [1943], December 23, 1943, Wright Papers; *Independent*, July 5, 1935; Crouch, *Bishop's Boys*, 523.

51. W. J. Tate to Orville Wright, November 30, 1947, Wright Papers; *News and Observer*, February 12, 1948; Crouch, *Bishop's Boys*, 524. Tate's letter of November 13 is not preserved among the Wright Papers.

52. *Daily Advance*, February 2, 1948; Saunders, "Then We Quit Laughing."

53. Etheridge interview; "Two Old Timers," 16; W. J. Tate to Orville Wright, October 12, 1937, Wright Papers.

54. Daniel Grady Tate, telephone interview with author, March 24, 1993; *News and Observer*, February 29, 1952.

55. Tate, "W. J. Tate and Family," 420-421; W. J. Tate to Fred C. Kelly, October 28, November 1, December 5, 1951, Wright Papers. Kelly reposed little faith in his North Carolina sources. He complained to an associate that Daniels had given out an account of the first flight "with such inaccuracy as to be downright silly" and that Johnny Moore "has always been considered a bit light in the head." As to Bill Tate, "[a]t least half of what he told me was untrue." See Fred C. Kelly to Lister D. Gardner, December 8 (undated), in CW-93000-06, Documents on Wright Brothers, National Air and Space Museum Library.

56. D. G. Tate, "Thomas Douglas Tate," "Elijah Tate," 418-419; Archie McLean, "An Outer Banks Tail of Woe," undated *News and Observer* clipping in possession of D. G. Tate.

57. *Morning Herald*, May 10, 1970; *Hattie Creef* file, Dare County Public Library, Manteo.

Index